D1481959

THE

By Hal Burton

THE CITY STRIKES BACK
THE SKI TROOPS

SKI TROOPS

HAL BURTON

Simon and Schuster · New York

356
B974s

To Minnie Dole,
WHO CREATED THE ARMY'S MOST UNUSUAL DIVISION,
AND THUS MADE THIS BOOK POSSIBLE

CONTENTS

1

The Lonely Places

IT IS RARELY NIGHT in the high mountains. Almost always, there is some reflection from the sky—except when the massed clouds pour in, enveloping the summits in a woolly curtain, rolling down into the valleys like a silent, impalpable avalanche. On a glacier or a snowfield, the tiniest sliver of moon, the faintest glimmer of stars, creates a dim, enduring twilight. Given such conditions, men who know the mountains move boldly. They evade the shadowed crevasses, deep canyons in a riven torrent of ice; they walk confidently beneath spired seracs, transformed from tottering pinnacles into frozen immobility by the chill of evening. Through the soles of their cleated climbing boots, they can sense literally every change and every danger in a dreamlike terrain almost as featureless as the surface of the moon.

With the coming of day, the glacier undergoes a transformation. It becomes a desert of snow and ice, perpetually in movement, perpetually in change. The sun, a burning corolla, floods the peaks with light and warmth. Hanging glaciers, suspended from the cliffs, crack and thunder hollowly as great chunks of ice break loose. Rocks rattle intermittently: The glacial mainstream is gnawing at the cliffs that confine it. The medial and lateral moraines, rivers of stone and gravel, flow down atop the snow,

9

moving as imperceptibly as the glacier itself. Where the glacier ends, so do these stony rivers, piling up in towering mounds of detritus, a jumble of barrenness in a barren landscape. Melting waters, milky with silt, pour out from the glacial tongue in a roaring torrent. Sound has replaced silence.

These are the lonely places of the world, but not the only ones. Such lonely places lie under the mountains as well as on them— in the high, sparse country where the trees dwindle to pigmy size at timberline; on the Alpine meadows bright with flowers and alive with the high, piping whistle of the marmot; and in the deep canyons where the torrents foam and thunder.

There are other lonely places, to be found wherever the rhythm of the seasons calls down the snow, and the stars snap like fragments of fire in a sky veiled, now and then, by the wavering green curtain of the Northern Lights. Norway, Sweden, Finland and Russia; the North American prairies and the ice-encased lakes of the Laurentian Shield; the forested mountains of the northeastern United States, some rising into the tundra climate of Labrador—all are tinged with this sense of loneliness. The camper who wakes at night to hear the wavering call of a loon across a remote northern lake, the cowboy searching for lost cattle in the teeth of a prairie blizzard, and the skier plummeting down a mountainside in a spray of powder snow share this loneliness and the challenge it poses, the mastery of a strange, forbidding setting in which hazard and discomfort must be faced and conquered.

The related sports of mountaineering and skiing have developed as one response. Beginning as man's private war against a hostile environment, they have from time to time become an instrument of war itself. Great mountain masses, along with forests and plains too deep in snow for soldiers to move on foot, offer an opportunity to outflank the enemy, to harass and bewilder him, to provide the distraction that enables the main force of an attacking army to reach its objectives unhindered by unexpected raids. The ski, which dates back at least to 2500 B.C., has been used in war since the thirteenth century A.D., when a soldier schussed downhill through the army besieging Slotsberg, in Scandinavia, carrying a call for help to reinforcements outside the encircled village. King Sverre of Norway (1184–1202) sent out a captain and company on skis to reconnoiter enemy positions before he won the Battle of Oslo.

By A.D. 1555, King Gustavus Vasa of Sweden was boasting that his ski troops could travel one hundred miles in a day. That same year, he ordered them into the Karelian Isthmus of Finland, against the Russians, "not to engage a superior enemy in open country but to lure them into forest ambush." The technique he devised was still effective against the same Russian enemy during the Finno-Russian winter war of 1939–1940.

Skiing traveled around the world with the Scandinavians, but in the beginning it was "cross-country" skiing, travel over rolling terrain. Hills were avoided as much as possible; when they had to be descended the system was to drag a long pole as a brake, or simply to fall down if braking didn't work. Norwegians introduced skiing to Australia in the mid-nineteenth century. They were miners imported to work the gold deposits. By the same time, Norwegians who had joined the gold rush to California were astounding native Americans with their skill on snow. John A. ("Snowshoe") Thomson carried the mail on skis from Placerville across the passes of the Sierra Nevada, a trip of nearly a hundred miles. Thomson used twelve-foot skis, so long, heavy and ungainly that he could only run straight downhill. He never knew that in Norway, some thirty years earlier, a technique of turning on skis to change direction and reduce speed had been developed. Modern skiing is merely an elaboration of that discovery.

Those inveterate travelers, the English, were the first to make skiing an international sport, and by the 1890s were astonishing the natives of St. Moritz with their agility. It took only a short time before all the Alpine nations of Europe had developed their own expert skiers. In 1903 the French established a Military Ski School for their mountain troops, the Chasseurs Alpins. In 1908 Switzerland, Norway, Sweden, France and Finland took part in the first International Military Patrol Race on skis. "Downhill" skiing, the art of descending steep slopes under control, still was regarded as too difficult for soldiers, but in Austria a revolution was in the making. The first ski school in Europe had been established there sixteen years earlier. Austrian techniques had devised the V-shaped snowplow as a new method of braking speed; and in 1907 Hannes Schneider started his own ski school in St. Anton, Austria. Schneider made skiing easy, and made it fun as well, by devising a step-by-step progression from the snowplow to the high-speed christiania turn, done on steep slopes with skis parallel. Before long, all the wealthy sportsmen of Great Britain and continental Europe were making the pilgrimage to St. Anton, whose reputation as a winter sports center has never diminished. The Austrian Army, much of it already trained in rudimentary skiing, adapted his technique, and Schneider himself was to see it put into practice in World War I.

The growth of mountaineering was much more steady and much less spectacular. The golden age of climbing had already been reached by the 1850s and 1860s. Determinedly acrobatic Englishmen—"muscular Christians" by the definition of Arnold of Rugby—laid siege to one seemingly inaccessible peak after another and conquered them all. This was warfare on the grand scale. Men such as Alfred Wills and Edward Whymper performed prodigies and sometimes took part in tragedies. Whymper's first ascent of the Matterhorn led to the death of a guide and two English climbing companions when the rope broke. The English newspapers were filled with bitter letters of condemnation, and even Queen Victoria asked her Prime Minister if something could be done to stop young men from risking their lives. But the very danger of mountaineering appealed to a venturesome generation, and climbing became—as it remains—the supreme sport and the ultimate challenge.

The English climbed only for sport, and the great Swiss guides who accompanied them climbed only for pay. The concept of the mountains as a military battlefield was totally alien to them. To be sure, Hannibal and Napoleon had crossed the Alps in opposing directions to win great military victories, but they came through the passes, along established routes. Around the turn of the last century, it dawned on all the Alpine nations that the peaks were as important as the passes. Skilled troops could fight across the summits, reconnoiter enemy dispositions from rocky aeries, and outflank the road-bound troops with their cumbersome transport. The French transformed their Chasseurs from small scouting forces to massed divisions. The Austro-Hungarians laid emphasis on their Alpenjäger, the Italians developed the Alpini, and the Swiss their mountain troops. In every case, there were mountain boundaries to protect.

Switzerland, except on the Rhine frontier, was hemmed in by the Alps. Germany's Bavarian frontier bordering Austria was Alpine, and only her own Alpine troops could man it. The Savoy Alps and the Dauphiné Alps separated France from Italy. Austria-Hungary had the Carpathian Alps and the Tatra as a barrier against the Russians, and on the Italian border overlooked the Venetian and Po Plains from the bristling peaks of the Dolomite, Carnic and Friulian Alps. The Russians had no mountain troops as such, but they did have ski troops, including the exceptional Finns. However, because of "political unreliability," the Finns were barred from frontline service.

The grand bloodletting of World War I was concentrated in the marshes and hedgerows of northern France and Belgium, but along most of the mountain boundaries where the Allies confronted the Central Powers both ski and Alpine troops saw action. Before Alsace-Lorraine was overrun by the Germans, the Chasseurs fought a series of brave actions on skis in the low, forested Vosges during the winter of 1914–1915. That same winter the Russians were decisively beaten by Austro-German Jäger on the Carpathian front. These Jäger now were free to take part in the most remarkable mountain war ever fought, the war in the Dolomite Alps.

From the Resia Pass, where the boundaries of Austria, Switzerland and Italy still meet, the Austro-Italian frontier in 1915 swept 40 miles southward in a great arc across the glaciers and perpetual snow of the Ortler group. It swung east to cross the head of Lake Garda below Trent, and boldly stormed the limestone spires of the Dolomites. Then it turned south again high above the Isonzo River and a town named Caporetto before losing itself in the coastal marshes of the Adriatic Sea some 75 miles east of Venice and 20 miles west of Trieste, the great Austrian naval base. This forbidding frontier, with its many twists and turns, stretched some 375 miles. Except for about 20 miles at the extreme eastern end, the whole length was a natural fortress, bastioned by the cliffs, canyons and glaciers of the Southern Alps. These lands had been taken from Italy by Austria in 1815, and probably most of the inhabitants were of Germanic stock. But to Italy it was territory that had been forcibly ripped away. The physical presence of Austrian military garrisons on the heights overlooking both the Po and Venetian plains was resented both as an insult and as a threat to most of northern Italy.

Conrad von Hötzendorff, the Austrian Chief of General Staff, had long been anticipating a war. His garrison troops on the Alpine front had spent years in preparation. The historian Luigi Villari wrote that the Trentino, which included the Dolomites, "had been converted into a vast fortress many years before; every mountain and every essential vantage point bristled with guns and was protected by elaborate fortifications with steel-plated domes. . . . Many hundreds of caverns had been dug out of the rocks (there were 300 of them in the Trentino alone) and the natural ones had been used and exploited to the fullest extent . . . in a word, nothing had been neglected to create a complete and organic system of defenses." Austrian guns covered every avenue of approach into the mountains.

The Italians had not been so forehanded. Italy was still a young nation and a weak one, plagued by a series of inadequate governments and bled by a recent disastrous military defeat in Libya. Its leaders hoped desperately not to be pulled into the war, and had made only minimal preparations. Italy, therefore, remained neutral when the guns of August 1914 began to fire. Behind the scenes, she was actively bargaining both with the Allies and with the Central Powers. The Allies offered better terms—the return of all the lands Italy had lost to Austria, plus other tempting concessions. On this basis, Italy signed a secret treaty with the Allies and declared war on Austria on May 23,

1915. A million and a half men faced each other across the highest battlefront of any war.

Neither von Hötzendorff nor his opposite number, General Luigi Cadorna, Chief of the Italian General Staff, proposed to make their main effort in the mountains. Their heaviest troop concentrations were on the twenty miles of lowland frontier along the Isonzo. If the Austrians broke through to the Adriatic, Venice would fall and Italy very probably would have to sue for peace. If the Italians broke through to Trieste, the home port of the Austrian Navy would be captured, the Austrian fleet would be out of action, and the Italian advance might continue into Serbia, menacing Austria's southern flank.

But armies have to protect all flanks, and the flanks that counted were in the Alps, from the stony, waterless foothills overlooking the Isonzo to the snow and ice peaks overhanging the Resia Pass. The thunder of cannon and the crack of machine-gun fire echoed and re-echoed among the Dolomite spires. It rumbled hollowly on the glaciers of the Ortler and the Adamello, the latter at 10,000 feet altitude the highest on the frontier. On the Carso Plateau overlooking the Isonzo, described by one Italian writer as "a howling wilderness of stones sharp as knives," the Austrians held firm and barred the way to Trieste. On the Mrzli, farther up the river, the 12th Bersagliere, not expert in mountaineering but bravely determined, stormed the cliffs only to lose 400 men, most of whom fell to their death before the Austrian positions finally were overrun. On Sleme, another strategic high point, the Cividale Alpine Battalion was stopped in its climbing boots just below the summit—not by machine guns but by a hail of stones thrown down by the Austrian garrison.

The Dolomites are renowned among climbers for their sheer cliffs and tiny but solid hand- and foot-holds that permit prodigies of climbing—"of the sixth grade," as mountaineers catalogue many of the most extreme routes. The sixth grade used to be considered the ultimate in rock climbing, but up through channels in the rock the soldiers of two armies put ropes in place as an aid to men carrying heavy packs, moved up their machine guns, and made their bivouacs on airy platforms where a misstep meant a certain plunge to death. Peaks that are famous today among mountaineers and skiers were familiar place names to Italians and Austrians in World War I. The Cristallo and the Tofana, above the winter resort of Cortina d'Ampezzo; the great triple towers of the Tre Cime di Lavaredo above Misurina; and the glaciers and ruddy cliffs of the 10,000-foot Marmolada all figured in the mountain war. There never has been so spectacular a battlefront. In the Dolomites, pine forests rise up from the valley floor to green Alpine meadows, and from these meadows the rock towers rise into the sky—brown and gray during the day, turning a flaming red as the sun begins to set. Every mountain pass is a cul de sac, and behind each range there is another, a tumbled sea of mountains boiling up to the topmost Alps and then subsiding into the valleys of the Austrian Tyrol. On these heights, as one historian noted, "peaks and positions could be held by a handful of men with a few machine guns against whole enemy brigades."

The mountain war was a grim war. By the estimate of historians for the U.S. Army Ground Forces, more men were killed in climbing accidents and avalanches than by gunfire. The sheer size of the two armies, essential to garrison a frontier of such length, meant that lowland soldiers had to be used to "beef up" the elite Alpini and Jäger divisions, which comprised less than one fifth of the total fighting force. During the winters of 1915 and 1916 whole battalions unskilled in the hazards of the mountains were wiped out by avalanches. The more knowledgeable ski troops avoided avalanche country. They knew what to watch for—unstable cornices that could split away, bringing down tons of snow with them; slopes covered with new-fallen snow that would slide when sliced by a ski track; telltale depressions in the snow that marked crevasses, some of them hundreds of feet deep. They stole silently into the enemy lines at night, made sudden raids, and as silently returned with prisoners to their bivouacs before sunrise. The very crevasses that could trap them often served as shelter wherever these clefts in the glacial ice were shallow enough to be reached by ladder. Less experienced troops shivered in wood and tin shelters, vulnerable to machine-gun and artillery fire, but the mountain troops lived snug in their snow caves.

The winter of 1916 brought home the unforgiving nature of the Alps to soldiers who had come from as far away as Sicily and Hungary. Rain and chilling fog in the valleys, and snow on the heights combined to make fighting one long agony. In its own strange way and its own odd setting, this war at the top of the Italian peninsula was a precursor to the war fought, lower down on the same peninsula, between Allies and Germans from 1943 to 1945. There were the same almost-breakthroughs that never quite succeeded; there was the same bitter weather; but in both cases the Italian Theater was overshadowed by events in France. Ypres, Passchendaele, the Marne and the Somme—these were the military spectaculars of World War I. Down in the mountains, the Austrians very nearly broke out from their Dolomite fortress onto the Italian plain, but they were stopped at the Asiago Plateau as, one war later, the Americans and British were stopped at Cassino. Vicenza lay just twenty-five miles away from Asiago; Vicenza was never reached. The Italians smashed through the passes above Cortina d'Ampezzo and reached the mountaintops in sight of Toblach, but they could never fight their way downhill to cut the main Austrian railroad line into the Dolomites.

This was a war of moles as well as of mountaineers. Sappers tunneled diligently into the porous limestones, audible to soldiers on the surface. They set off vast explosions under the feet of enemy garrisons. One such blast, undertaken by the Austrians, blew the whole top off the Col di Lan, and made a national hero of the Austrian general who managed the operation. But what the world does remember about the Italian campaign is not this bitter, unrewarding military seesaw. It is a town called Caporetto.

The Italians by 1917 were holding the whole valley of the Isonzo as far north as the village of Plezzo, more than forty miles above the Adriatic. Six German divisions, all of them backed by Jäger battalions from the Bavarian Alps, had been added to the Austrian Fourteenth Army and hidden from sight in the canyons above Caporetto. One of these battalions came from Württemberg and was commanded by a young major named Erwin Rommel. The daring he displayed was to win him promotion within the German Army and worldwide attention some twenty-five years later in the North African desert. At 8:00 A.M., October 24, with mist shrouding the valleys and wet snow pelting the Italian garrisons on the mountain slopes, the Austro-German attack began. By midafternoon, a fifteen-mile gap had been punched in the Isonzo Line.

The main Austro-German force poured down the valley while the mountain troops "took to the tops," and overran one position after another. Rommel's force, scaling the cliffs, outflanked a mountain battalion from Trent. Its commander, weeping with rage, reluctantly surrendered his troops. The Alpini and Bersaglieri on those heights could not have fought more bravely, but the lowland divisions simply dissolved. They felt themselves an even match for the Austrians, but they were simply terrified of the relentless Germans. Ernest Hemingway has told the human story of the rout in *A Farewell to Arms*. The Italians did not run, as assumed by their aggravated allies in France and England. They simply downed arms and strolled away. Caporetto initiated the legend that Italians were cowardly soldiers, but that was hardly true. The home front was collapsing behind them. Short of food and weary of the whole struggle, the Italian people were rising up in riots.

Yet enough soldiers were loyal at Caporetto so that General Cadorna was able to retire in order, with much of his army intact, behind the river line of the Piave forty miles west. Two French divisions and three English divisions, pulled from the battle lines in France, gave the Italians the strength to stay on the Piave until October 1918. Austria itself, desperately weary of the war, was already signaling for an armistice. The old Emperor Franz Josef, the last symbol of national unity, had died on November 21, 1916. His successor, the Archduke Karl, had no stomach for further fighting, for the Austro-Hungarian Empire was in turmoil. Italian attacks routed the Austrians at the Battle of Vittorio Veneto; the front simply evaporated; and on November 4, 1918, Austria and Italy signed an armistice.

This was the first great mountain war. Very possibly it will be the last. Yet in its own strange, unnoticed fashion, it was perhaps the ultimate vindication of human resolution: Evidence of the prodigies the individual can accomplish when the cruelties of war join forces with the cruelties of nature. The rusted helmets still hang from the barbed wire on the Col di Lan. The great limestone cliffs above Caporetto, from which green waterfalls leap into space, still show the scars of caverns that once housed Austrian guns. The patient searcher along the Dolomite battle line can still find the old dugouts, tenanted now by foxes and snakes. Except for Caporetto, this is a forgotten war, but it deserves a better memorial than that invidious name—for it was here that mountain warfare vindicated itself, at a cost of 680,000 Italian lives and almost as many among the Austrians.

THE WINTER WAR

Skis were an oddity and combat in the snow was arcane during World War I, but by 1939 great changes had occurred. Aerial tramways, perfected during 1914–1918 to bring supplies to troops high on the mountainsides, were further developed to carry skiers to even greater altitudes. The whole of the Alps, including the Dolomites, became a great winter playground. The first Winter Olympics, at Chamonix in 1924, dramatized the challenge of skiing. The second, at Lake Placid in 1932, awakened Americans to the sport. The newspapers, intrigued by this curious sport with its hint of danger, devoted columns of text and pictures to it. The total number of Americans who skied was trivial in comparison to the popularity, but millions of Americans knew what skiing was.

On November 30, 1939, the second war on skis began. Russia, a nation of 190,000,000 population, attacked Finland, a nation of barely 3,000,000. Few Americans had known about the Dolomite war—it was effectively upstaged by the grim nature of the trench warfare in France and Belgium, where United States troops saw battle. Even fewer remembered the dispatch of a handful of American and British regiments to Murmansk directly after World War I, in an effort to save White Russian forces from defeat by the Communist army. One British regiment brought skis to Murmansk, and there was plenty of movement over snow, but the Allied forces accomplished little, and the whole intervention was a failure, to be forgotten quickly.

Long before this, Americans had fought on snow. During the French and Indian War, the Colonists learned that the Indians were most vulnerable in winter. They disliked traveling during the bad weather, and if they staged raids they could be tracked to their villages. On March 11, 1703, the order was issued that there be "500 pairs of good snowshoes provided at the public charge, 125 pairs thereof to be put into the hands of each Colonel or chief military officer of the regiments of militia within the county of Hampshire, the North Regiment of Middlesex, the North Regiment of Essex, and the regiment in the county of Yorke, lying frontier next the wilderness, to be in readiness for His Majesty's service."

There were more than enough recruits for this demanding duty. The Province of Massachusetts approved bounties ranging from ten to fifty pounds for each Indian scalp. The "snowshoe men" were heroes in their communities. At least nine companies had been organized by 1725, and they kept the frontier relatively quiet. By 1743 there were thirteen companies, but when the Colonists and British captured the fortress of Louisburg in June 1745, a temporary peace came to the Colonies, and the snowshoe men faded into history. Even the American army had forgotten them; the Finnish war seemed unique when actually its tactics and terrain were as old as the history of this country.

What made the Russo-Finnish War so dramatic was the disparity in strength between the two sides. A giant country was attacking a tiny one, and taking an unmerciful beating. Finns on skis were outranging, outflanking and baffling a highly mechanized Russian Army attacking in traditional fashion along the few roads that crossed the Russo-Finnish border. The Russians attacked at three separate points. They bypassed the heavily fortified Mannerheim Line across the Karelian Isthmus, hoping that victory farther north would save them the cost of a frontal assault. But the country was not easy. Finland is a land of rolling hills, interminable forests and winding streams, with 60,000 lakes as an added barrier to invasion. To anyone but a Finn, it is almost impenetrable. The Finns, however, knew how to cope with such forbidding winter terrain. They knew how to move through the forests, how to bivouac in the spruce thickets, protected from bitter winds, how to build a fire from birch bark and the boughs of conifers, and how to care for themselves in weather that often dropped to 60 degrees below zero Fahrenheit.

The Russians by contrast hugged the roads. They sent out scarcely any patrols to protect long columns of tanks, armored cars, trucks, field kitchens and motorized artillery. The Finns simply melted into the forest on their skis. At one point on the border there was nothing to oppose them but a patrol of 60 frontier guards. These resourceful men shot from ambush, immobilizing the motorized columns, and raced on skis from position to position. The Red Army commander reported to Moscow that he was being attacked by vastly superior forces.

The Finns concentrated their attacks on brigade headquarters and field headquarters, leaving the command forces to face hunger and cold. Silently, stealthily, they built winter roads parallel to the Red columns on the main highways. Such roads, used by lumbermen in all northern countries, were dotted with stumps, sawed close to the ground. When water was poured over the stumps and snow shoveled around them, the result was a hard-frozen surface over which the Finns could move forward their own motorized equipment. Every two miles or so, along these winter roads, the Finns cleared paths to the highways and fell upon the Russians. By the second week in January, the Reds' principal thrust along the highway from Suomossalmi had ended in disaster: 36,000 Russians were dead and fewer than 15,000 Finns. Midway up the Russo-Finnish border another two Russian divisions had been as effectively shattered.

The Finns fought in white camouflage clothes; the Russians in khaki uniforms, a stark traget against the snow, doomed "like Arctic foxes that had not developed a winter coat." Everything the Finns fired or carried was white; Russian guns and trucks were the normal, utilitarian color of military equipment around the world. The Finns camped in dugouts roofed with logs and skins. Their stoves burned wood that gave off no smoke or sparks to reveal where troops were encamped. The Russians, numbed by the cold and terrified by the black vastness of the nighttime forest, huddled around blazing fires—easy targets for the Finnish scouts. In an odd way, it was like the French and Indian Wars along the American frontier—the greater power fighting a conventional war, the outnumbered enemy using stealth and surprise as a paralyzing riposte.

The Russians had ski troops of their own, but they had been trained on the open plains, and with equipment designed for such travel. For skin bindings, they used the traditional toe plate and heel strap created for high-altitude ski troops in World War I. By contrast, the Finns used narrow cross-country skis, to which the boots were attached only at the toe. In a fire fight, the Finnish skis could be kicked off quickly, enabling soldiers to move into the most effective firing position. The Russians were trapped in their cumbersome bindings, unable to get them off quickly. Their desperate predicament finally led to air drops of more suitable equipment, but most of the parachuted equipment fell into Finnish hands. The Russian commanders called for more ski troops, and on February 15, 1940, a ski brigade from Siberia went into action. Accustomed to fighting in the open, the soldiers skied boldly out onto a lake. A torrent of fire descended from all directions. Every man in the brigade was killed.

By now the British and French had decided to send volunteers, and at least one American joined the Finns. David T. Bradley, a distinguished American downhill ski racer and ski jumper, the son of a University of Wisconsin professor, served with the Finnish Army as an observer. His acute comments on the specialized nature of the war and the usefulness of soldiers on skis helped to stimulate interest among American skiers as well as the few officers in the War Department at Washington who recognized that the United States might someday have to fight on snow again.

Eventually, good sense dawned on the Russians. They could

not fight and win a winter war under the conditions prevailing in Finland. Their military reputation was badly damaged: How could one of the great powers, with such masses of men and material, suffer so many defeats by a tiny country with only minimum manpower and equipment? The Soviet generals then did what they should have done in the first place. They staged a frontal attack against the Mannerheim Line on the Karelian Isthmus and at the same time sent men and equipment across the frozen ice of the Gulf of Finland to outflank it. The Finns— gallant beyond all reason—fought to the end, but on March 13, 1940, they signed a peace treaty that ceded much of the Karelian Isthmus, plus the fortress of Viborg, to the Russians. The war was over. Men and machines had overwhelmed a brave people.

England and the United States both learned a lesson, though only a tentative one, from the Finnish war. The Imperial General Staff began the training of ski troops in Scotland. The General Staff of the United States Army created six ski patrols from its experienced draftees—two on the East Coast, two in the Midwest, and two in the West. Among military men, the faint suspicion was growing that ski troops, if not mountain troops, might be useful to have on hand if a second world war broke out.

2

The Age of Innocents

AMERICAN INFATUATION with mountains and snow grew out of two unrelated occurrences, one staggering in its impact, the other almost anonymous. The first of these was the Depression, which effectively discredited the pursuit of wealth and enforced a simpler life on almost everyone. The second was the invention by a Swiss engineer of an odd little device called the rope tow. This motorized creation, operating with an endless rope, permitted skiers to ride up small hills that previously had to be climbed, thereby taking some of the work out of the sport. It appealed to the American reliance on machinery as a substitute for physical effort.

By fortunate coincidence the new President was a man with a passion for parks and wilderness. He had climbed the eastern mountains and camped in the eastern woods until immobilized by polio. One of Franklin D. Roosevelt's first actions was to establish the Civilian Conservation Corps, an agency created to take jobless boys off the streets and into the state and national parks. Once there, they cleared footpaths, built public campsites —and in the Northeast, the Rockies and the Far West moved on to chop ski trails through the forests and down the mountainsides. Along with the rope-tow riders, skiers with the strength, the will, and the proper equipment now could climb up through the frosty woods, experience the windswept beauty of the high country, and come downhill on broad, curving lanes through the timber.

This wasn't Alpine skiing, to be sure, except in a few of the western parks, but it had its own sense of adventure, spiced by special perils. The skier who missed a turn, if traveling at any speed, would end up in the bordering forest with a sprained ankle or a broken leg as the penalty. It was sport for the tough-minded. The racers from Dartmouth, Harvard, Yale and Williams, from the universities of New Hampshire, Vermont and Washington, plunged down the mountain trails at terrific speeds. By 1936 America was able to enter a men's ski team in the Alpine events of the Winter Olympics at Garmisch-Partenkirchen. There was a women's team, too, a collection of girls in short skirts and high red stockings. The downhill courses were icy; the slaloms, where racers must pass through pairs of flags, were appallingly difficult by American standards. Neither team won any Olympic medals, but both did establish that Alpine ski racing was no longer a European monopoly. Dick Durrance, a Dartmouth racer, astounded the Europeans by placing eleventh in the downhill, eighth in the slalom, and tenth in the combined results.

This was, of course, the second phase of American skiing. Norwegian immigrants brought ski jumping to the United States in 1887. In that year a Norwegian named Mikkel Hemmestvedt executed the first tournament jump on American soil, soaring 57 feet from a hillside in Red Wing, Minnesota. Because it looks more dangerous than it really is, jumping appeals to the blood-thirsty strain that hides behind the American zest for spectator sports. There have never been more than a few thousand ski jumpers in the United States at any given time. The jumpers themselves, until recent years, were on the average simple laboring men. They were a hard-drinking, loud-singing, swaggering, convivial crew who devoted their weekends and holidays to the art of flying, so to speak, without wings. A good many of the pre-World War II jumpers could not operate effectively without a little stimulant. These bibulous worthies, too numerous to name, could carry a half-pint bottle of whiskey to the top of the jumping hill, drain it while waiting to start, and then kick off into space enveloped in a happy haze of bourbon.

Until the 1930s, with few exceptions, American skiing consisted solely of ski jumping and cross-country racing on skis. The national jumping championships were established in 1904; the Dartmouth Outing Club, founded in 1907, brought jumping and cross-country into the college circuit. Downhill skiing was still unknown in 1932 when the Winter Olympics, held at Lake Placid, first made the nation aware that it was possible to have an enjoyable time out-of-doors when the temperature dropped below freezing. These Olympics, so to speak, acted as a seedbed for downhill skiing, which so quickly became a participant sport.

The combination of toughness and skill required to ski the mountains appealed to a growing number of outdoorsmen outside the colleges. At most, there may have been 10,000 skiers by 1935. They were concentrated on the northeastern seaboard, in the Colorado Rockies, the Pacific Northwest, and in California, all areas where the mountains were reasonably close at hand. They were immersed in the creation of new trails, the opening of new slopes, the discovery of new mountains deep in untracked powder snow—or, in the East, often glittering with ice so solid that a downhill run was a slide for life. Ski equipment from Europe had begun to appear in the shops: wooden skis with steel edges, which held better on the turns; rigid metal toeplates into which the ski boot was jammed; leather straps encircling the heel of the boot and fitting into a slot in the heel. In the mid-thirties came the cable binding, with a spring around the heel that could be snapped tight, holding the boot irrevocably to the ski. In a fall, sometimes the heel cable stretched and the skier escaped injury. More often it didn't, and the result was a sprain or a fracture. The motto of those rough-and-tumble days was, "Thou must not fall"—for if "thou" did, nobody knew how to administer first aid, and it often took hours before a rescuer appeared with a toboggan to drag you down to the highway and to drive you to the nearest doctor's office.

This was the era of ski wax, a messy substance that stuck to the hands and clothes, and now and then to the soles of the skis. The purpose of waxing was to make it possible to climb reasonably steep slopes without slipping back. By some mysterious alchemy, the skier could come down the same slopes without sticking.

A pleasant odor of pine tar accompanied the waxing process, but that was about the extent of the pleasure. The wax, softened to room temperature, would be rubbed on and then smoothed with a block of cork. Sometimes a hot iron would be applied to melt the wax more evenly, an effective method if one discounts the liquid wax that dripped on rugs and floors and solidified there. A good job of waxing could win a race for a skier; a bad job could ruin the day for him. Waxing was, and still is, one of the great challenges of the sport. It appealed to the scientist in every American, just as the changes, improvements and new inventions in ski equipment appealed to the gadgeteers, for snow conditions very often differ according to altitude, and the skier at the bottom would have to estimate the kinds of snow he would find as he climbed. Sometimes a mountain might have three types of snow between the bottom and the top. Knowledgeable skiers could put on exactly enough of each type of wax so that one layer wore through to the next as the snow changed, and then all gave way to a hard base wax for a fast run to the bottom.

All of these tangibles and intangibles—the mystery of mountains and snow, the demands on physical strength and emotional courage, the sense of newness, the specialized equipment—produced an inner core of American skiers with unparalleled devotion to the sport. They gave skiing a motive and purpose it has never lost, even in an era of mechanization when millions ski. To them, as to Otto Schniebs, the great German-born ski teacher and former Dartmouth coach, "Skiing is not just a sport; it is a way of life." But in the thirties they were not much inclined to impart that special way of life to outsiders. Skiing was, so to speak, a WASP sport. Its attitudes and its codes of etiquette ("one calls TRACK! when passing another skier on the trail; if one falls, and makes a hole in the trail, one stamps it level before going on") were based on the guidelines provided by the elite Ski Club of Great Britain. That rather elegant organization was founded by Sir Arnold Lunn, inventor of the slalom and tireless propagandist for the sport. The British *Ski Yearbook* was the New Testament of inner American skiing, and English skiing became the model for Americans to follow. Thus, while a certain number of hearty, uninhibited ski clubs developed across the United States, the leadership was provided by gentlemanly clubs such as the Amateur of New York and the Hochgebirge of Boston. These associations recruited so many members of the Social Register that it was unnecessary to ask anyone's antecedents. It was a little like the period before Queen Victoria when members of the peerage were fewer and introductions were pointless because everyone knew everyone. The Amateurs and the Hochgebirges established new ski races, provided new trophies, and tirelessly hunted for new mountains where—hopefully —the snow was more reliable and where state or local governments could be prevailed upon to clear ski trails.

But on the periphery of skiing, there were already portents of change, the first of which was the rope tow. The first of these, based on a Swiss invention, opened in 1932 at Shawbridge, in the Laurentian Mountains of Quebec. Soon the word spread that it was possible to ride up a hillside instead of climbing it. In 1934, the first tow in the United States was installed on Gilbert's Hill, a steep pasture slope at Woodstock, Vermont. It was a simple device, like all those that followed. An endless rope, on the average 750 feet long but sometimes extending to 1,000 feet, was stretched over a series of flanged wheels attached to poles. Power came from a gasoline motor, generally scavenged from an old Ford. The wheels were old automobile tire rims. Skiers wore heavy gloves to protect their hands. They stepped up to the moving rope, gripped it tightly, and took off with a lurch. Now and then a thoughtless skier who had failed to check on his parka found it twisted into the rope and himself being carried inexorably into the machinery. Rope tow riding developed a generation of skiers with prehensile arms, but at least it did multiply the amount of downhill skiing possible within the short hours of a winter day.

By 1937 there were rope tows all over the Berkshires, Catskills, Adirondacks, Green and White Mountains in the East, and on many of the western mountains as well. One of these tows, set up on Mt. Baker, Washington, was described as the steepest in the United States. The description proved accurate. One morning, while the tow operator was revving up the motor, the whole mountainside avalanched. The body was recovered from fifteen feet of snow. Another tow, possibly equally steep, established Woodstock, Vermont, as the Valhalla of early skiers. This tow rose up a hill so sheer that the bottom could not be seen from the top. The hill was named "Suicide Six." Bunny Bertram, the owner, ran the tow so fast that skiers arriving at the top were flung into space like bullets. At Pittsfield, Massachusetts, Claire Bousquet laced his gentler meadows with six tows. And there were plenty of easier ones around.

At last the masses found a reason to ski. It was no longer hard work and, on a slope, even the most chickenhearted had space to attempt a clumsy turn, or to fall down when the turn didn't succeed. The next step in the progress of skiing was inevitable, the snow train. Railroads were feeling the pinch of the Depression; passenger business had fallen off. Rather than permit passenger coaches and steam locomotives to stand idle on the sidings, the railroads went on the prowl for excursion business, and found it in the snow country. The Boston and Maine Railroad dispatched its first snow train from North Station, Boston, to the sheep meadows of Warner, New Hampshire, in 1931. Three years later, the New Haven Railroad sent trains to Norfolk, Connecticut, and then to Pittsfield and South Lee, Massachusetts. By 1942, when wartime austerity intervened, close to 100,000 skiers in the East, Midwest and West had traveled on the day excursion trains. These bargain excursions, at a maximum $2 to $2.50 round trip, were soon followed by overnight trains to bigger mountains and snowier hills. Skiing now commanded all the basic ingredients of success: uphill transportation, fast train service, and trails down the mountains.

The countryside added to the quality of the sport. The eastern trains chugged north all night, at daybreak stopping with a soft hiss of steam in little New England villages where white houses and red barns lay buried deep in snow. Farmhouses opened to house the visitors in frosty bedrooms where rime etched patterns on the window panes. Farm wives served up meals of staggering size, family style, around the kitchen table. There might be running water, but often the only privy was an outhouse in the back yard. The mountains, on a fine day, glittered against icy blue skies. Heavy snows bowed the trees, and soon the ski teachers were barking orders, usually in an Austrian accent, to dutiful students who wanted to master the snow and to ski the higher, steeper trails. It was a time of great innocence of spirit and jovial confusion. One morning Lowell Thomas, the radio commentator, woke just as his Rutland Railroad sleeper train was pulling into Manchester, Vermont. Thomas was an inveterate skier and a great traveler, who always took a coterie of friends with him. Barking orders, he dispatched two of the party to the baggage car for the skis. Since they didn't know whose skis belonged to whom, they pitched several dozen pairs out, and into a snowbank. For the rest of the day the Rutland station in Manchester was besieged by irate telephoners, demanding to know what had happened to their skis.

The teachers provided the backbone for the sport, and the resort owners the seedbed. There had been recreational skiing of a mild order at the Lake Placid Club, in upstate New York, since 1906, and semiformal instruction since the 1920s. But organized class instruction according to a standard system came to America much later. Peckett's, at Sugar Hill, New Hampshire, probably was the birthplace of the organized American ski school. Katherine Peckett, daughter of the owner, had skied while in boarding school in the Alps. In 1929 she persuaded her father to import two brilliant Austrian instructors, Kurt Thalhammer and Sig Buchmayr. Peckett's opened in winter that year for the first time, introducing to the United States the official Austrian technique of skiing. Buchmayr was a born showman and a notable propagandist for the sport. He sharpened interest in skiing by a series of acrobatic performances for the cameramen. One of these, a classic picture, showed him making a jump turn on the fifty-degree slopes of Tuckerman Ravine, a bowl on the eastern slope of Mt. Washington. He communicated the excitement of the sport better than any teacher since.

In fact, the first certified teacher to reach the United States had arrived without fanfare two years before Peckett's opened for winter. In 1927 Otto Schniebs, a former mountain trooper in Germany's World War I army, had come over from Swabia to work as a designer for the Waltham (Massachusetts) Watch Company. The first time he went down a hill on skis at a local golf course, he was spotted. By 1928 he was teaching skiing to members of the Appalachian Mountain Club, an influential association of hikers and climbers, and then to members of the Harvard Mountaineering Club. By 1930 the Dartmouth Outing Club had hired him as coach. Schniebs was a true missionary for skiing, an after-dinner speaker of rare quality. His astonishing misuse of the English language made him a prime favorite at outing club meetings and dinner parties. He greeted one group of Smith college students by saying, "Girls, I'm here to tell you when to do it and when not to do it . . . on skis."

On another occasion, an aspiring skier rose from the audience to ask, "Otto, what do I do if I find myself on a very narrow trail, and it's icy, and I'm scared?"

Schniebs replied, "Well, the only answer is to schtem like hell, or else take off the goddam t'ings and walk down."

A notable authority on waxing, he used this skill to win, of all things, a race on snowshoes. A snowshoe race between Dartmouth and the University of New Hampshire was an annual event. New Hampshire, which took only a minimal interest in the skiing events, always won the snowshoeing. Schniebs, assuming an innocent look, went to see the New Hampshire coach. "My boys," he said, "don't like the snowshoe race very much, and they haven't done very good in it. But suppose they win. Would you be willing to abolish the race?" The New Hampshire coach willingly assented. That night Schniebs stayed up late waxing the bottom of the snowshoes to be used by the Dartmouth team.

Dartmouth won the snowshoe race, and the event vanished from the winter carnival. The infuriated New Hampshire coach accused Schniebs of inserting nails in the snowshoe bottoms, and insisted upon inspecting them. He went away scratching his head; not only were there no nails, but there was not a trace of wax. It had all worn off. Schniebs kept his secret until the next winter carnival, when he revealed his legitimate duplicity.

Witty, lively and inspiring, Schniebs convinced thousands of Americans that skiing could be fun and that learning to ski need not be a chore. To Dartmouth he brought a quality of resolution and daring that made its racers unmatched throughout the 1930s, and created a generation of folk heroes for those just entering the sport. He was largely responsible for the first national downhill race, held in 1932 on an abandoned carriage road dropping from the summit of Mt. Moosilauke, New Hampshire. Trees and brush narrowed the road to a width of ten feet, and down this chute the racers careened. By some miracle no one was injured, and Henry Woods, a Dartmouth skier, won the national downhill championships.

From this old roadway, long since abandoned, came the concept of trails actually designed for skiing, cut wide enough to be reasonably safe when taken at high speed. These trails followed the contour of the ground, with curves at frequent intervals simulating the manner in which skiers changed direction on the limitless slopes of the Alps. The first such trail, laid out by Schniebs in 1933, was also on Mt. Moosilauke. It was named Hell's Highway and lived up to the title. At one point the trail was so steep that the thin soil cover eventually slid away, leaving only bare ledge rock. The next year Duke Dmitri von Leuchtenberg, another ski teacher, opened the Taft Racing Trail on Cannon Mountain, New Hampshire, the first to be cleared by the CCC. At Mt. Washington, Charles Proctor designed the John Sherburne Trail, descending from the Alpine bowl of Tuckerman Ravine to the highway at Pinkham Notch. The following year, 1935, the CCC cleared half a dozen trails in the Berkshires and the precipitous Nose Dive and Chin Clip trails at Mt. Mansfield. (Mildly alarming to downright frightening titles were the vogue of the era, spawning a whole generation of trails with such names as Shincracker, Plummet, and Guillotine, among others. Skiing still was considered a "tough" sport, and very little effort was exerted to lure the less experienced up the mountains.)

At Mansfield the Nose Dive and Chin Clip pulled in the experts, along with the somewhat easier Bruce Trail, but what really laid the foundation of success was the Mt. Mansfield Toll Road, a gentle and reasonably wide automobile road more than four miles long. On this long, pleasant run through the rime-frosted spruce and hardwoods, probably more beginning skiers developed a lasting devotion for the sport than on any other trail in the United States.

The teachers, so to speak, had created the terrain for the skiers. Next they initiated a complex discipline, the Arlberg technique, developed by Hannes Schneider in Austria. A godlike figure, before whom even kings like Michael of Rumania cringed, Schneider was as precise as a military commander, with his teachers as subofficers. When asked to establish branches of his school in the United States, he chose the best—managers who would not deviate an inch from his system. Otto Lang, a soft-spoken young man, went to the great Alpine slopes of Mts. Rainier and Baker, in Washington. Benno Rybizka, the son of a Czech general, was dispatched to Intervale, New Hampshire, and later moved down the road to North Conway. Luggi Foeger went to Yosemite National Park. Of the lot, Rybizka was most the martinet. A ski school student who absent-mindedly lit a cigarette while waiting his moment to show the teacher how well he could make turns would be banished from class, or at least given a tongue-lashing. Idle conversation was forbidden. Rybizka was there to give people their money's worth, whether they wanted it or not. But, in the process, he turned out some astoundingly good skiers.

America adopted the Arlberg technique as gospel, though learning it was a long and often frustrating process. First the student had to be shown how to carry his skis, then how to put them on. He learned two methods of walking on skis over level ground and two ways of climbing uphill. He learned how to come down gentle slopes, and then progressed to the V-position of the snowplow. Sometimes he never got out of it, to the undisguised amusement of Norwegian teachers like Erling Strom at Lake Placid Club, or the Swiss instructor Peter Gabriel at Franconia, both heretics where the Arlberg technique was concerned. From the snowplow, he went to the snowplow turn, to the stem turn, and then at long last to the stem christiania, a swing executed at high speed on steeper slopes. That, for most skiers, was reward enough, but a few went on to learn the parallel turn, executed with skis held tightly together. Now, as then, the parallel turn is the ultimate of the sport.

The king of ski teaching, Hannes Schneider himself, arrived in 1939. A devout Catholic, he was an opponent of Hitler and of anti-Semitism. The secretary of the Austrian Ski Federation was a Jew, and under attack long before Hitler annexed Austria to Germany. Despite heavy pressures, Schneider stood by him, remarking, "When X gave 10,000 Austrian marks [about $2,000] to the Ski Federation, everybody praised him. Now everybody attacks him. They forget what he did for skiing." The day of the Anschluss, Schneider was hustled out of his native St. Anton and placed in protective custody in a schoolhouse in Garmisch-Partenkirchen. The Arlberg-Kandahar races, one of the great events in world skiing, were to take place in St. Anton in a few days. Without consultation, as a tribute to Schneider, every foreign team except Germany withdrew from the races, which were cancelled.

Schneider owed his rescue to Harvey Dow Gibson, then president of the Manufacturers Trust Company in New York, who had created a new ski center on Cranmore Mountain in North Conway, his hometown. Gibson, by a skillful use of blocked German funds in foreign banks, made a deal with the Nazis, and Schneider was freed. Gibson never would say how much this cost him, but the sum was obviously substantial, for Schneider was one of the men in Austria most hated by the Austrian Nazi party. He arrived in North Conway to the pealing of church bells and the blare of a band, and walked out of the railroad station under an archway of ski poles. Yet the White Mountain countryside, so gentle by comparison with the Austrian Alps, came as a shock to him. After one sweeping look around, his glance passing over 6,223-foot Mt. Washington, he shyly inquired, "But where are the mountains?" Schneider died in 1955, but his ski school at North Conway still prospers under the direction of his son, Herbert.

Sometimes the Austrian teachers who came to America were racers as well, and one of them became a folk hero. Young Toni Matt, only nineteen, had been sent to North Conway by Schneider just before the Anschluss. After a series of successes in other races, he entered the toughest race of them all, the American Inferno. This ultimate in competition started at the top of Mt. Washington, dove down the headwall of Tuckerman Ravine, and then plunged down through the trees to Pinkham Notch—a vertical drop of 4,223 feet in about four miles. There were no lifts; skiers had to climb to the summit up the headwall. Matt had been in the ravine only once before, and that was on a day of dungeon fog when nothing could be seen. He had plenty of advice from other racers: Ski fast down the top part of the course, check your speed by turns over the 60-degree "lip" of the headwall, and then make three or four more turns on the headwall itself before straightening out for the run to the bottom.

Matt, as he puts it, came over the lip of the headwall so fast that he didn't dare to turn. Instead, he went straight down— "schussed" the headwall without a turn, hitting speeds up to 80 miles an hour. He completed the entire course in 6 minutes, 29 seconds. The next fastest runner, who had made turns, took far longer. It was the most astonishing performance American skiing ever had seen, and it made young Matt one of the great figures of the sport. He did more to demonstrate what speed, skill and daring could accomplish, when coupled with technical knowledge, than anyone else who has followed him.

By this time there were enough competent skiers so that a ski race was no longer a private event, watched only by racers and the personnel necessary to carry out the timing, slope preparation, and the marking of obstacles. In 1937 the Eastern Downhill Championships were transferred to Mt. Mansfield from Mt.

Greylock, Massachusetts, where the snow was insufficient. It was held on the Nose Dive, then as now one of the most demanding racing trails in the East. To everyone's astonishment, more than 2,000 spectators showed up. The narrow, muddy road down the mountain was so clogged with cars after the race that some motorists didn't reach the paved highway at Stowe until ten at night.

Skiing, it was obvious, was outgrowing the rope-tow stage. The search began for better ways to carry skiers longer distances up the mountainsides. Europe had plenty of aerial tramways as a prototype, to be sure, but just about all of these expensive devices for uphill transportation had been built at great cost by the governments of the various Alpine countries to encourage tourist trade. In America, where state and local governments didn't care this much about skiing, or didn't realize its potential, something more compact and less costly had to be found—something to fit the pocketbook of the private resort developer. First, as a result, came a new and far cheaper lift, the J-bar.

A Dartmouth professor, visiting the Alps, had stumbled upon a lift that was novel even in Europe, the T-bar. This lift utilized an endless steel cable and rigid towers. Lengths of a mile were possible. The rope tow, by contrast, could rarely be extended beyond 1,500 to 2,000 feet. The drag of the rope itself and the physical discomfort of the skier made greater lengths impossible. But with a T-bar, skiers were no longer yanked up the hill. Instead, they were pushed. They leaned back, two by two, against a wooden bar, an inverted "T" suspended from the cable, and were shoved uphill. The anonymous Dartmouth genius converted the T-bar into a J-bar, carrying just one skier at a time. The first of its type was erected on Oak Hill, near Hanover, seat of the college. Next the T-bar itself came to Pico Peak, Vermont, in 1936, imported by an enthusiastic young Vermont couple, Brad and Janet Mead. It was soon followed by the first aerial tramway in America, constructed by the state of New Hampshire at Cannon Mountain alongside Hawthorne's Great Stone Face.

The great liberation of American skiing was completed when Averell Harriman commissioned the first chair lift. Founder of

Sun Valley, Harriman was searching for some new type of uphill transportation that would carry more skiers than a tramway and at greater distances than a T-bar or J-bar. He assigned the job to engineers of the Union Pacific Railroad, of which he was president. One of these engineers, James Curran, had built aerial tramways in the tropics to carry bananas from the shore to the holds of ships lying offshore. Huge bunches of bananas were caught up on hooks attached to an overhead cable, and then disengaged to drop into the holds. Why not, mused Curran, substitute chairs for hooks? Skiers could move into position, sit in each chair, and be carried aloft, unloading themselves at the top of the lift by skiing out of the way. Harriman approved the innovation. The first two chair lifts in the world were set up on Dollar and Proctor Mountains at Sun Valley, and a new era for skiing had begun. In 1939, the first chair lift in the East went into service on Mt. Mansfield, and the old ski village of Stowe became the most important winter center on the Atlantic side of the Rockies.

By World War II, a sport viewed in the beginning as the private preserve of the rich had become the prerogative of hundreds of thousands of Americans.

3

The Age of Maecenas

AMERICAN SKIING never would have developed beyond its helter-skelter beginning without the help of wealthy patrons. Any farmer who could scrape together a thousand dollars was able to build a rope tow that provided him with a modest income during the slack winter months. But building a ski lift called for money far beyond the means of any local entrepreneur. That automatically narrowed the field to the rich. These were men with the funds to buy or lease whole mountainsides; men with money to cut trees, blast stumps, bulldoze hillsides and blow out rocks; often men with fortunes vast enough to construct whole ski resorts from scratch, complete with inns, shops, skating rinks, machinery to roll and pack the snow, and an employee payroll that ran to hundreds of thousands of dollars during a season of little more than three months.

As Maecenas in his time was the patron of the arts, so the rich in the mid-1930s became the patrons of skiing. There is something heady about dominating a whole mountain and bending it to one's will, something inspiring in transforming it from a tangle of trees and rocks into a disciplined complex of trails, slopes and uphill transportation devices. The patrons of skiing could afford this pleasure. They didn't have to worry whether the money they spent ever was repaid. In some cases, it was written off on the income tax return as a business loss. Shrewd men organized corporations and enrolled their friends as stockholders, thereby tying them irrevocably to the sport. As had earlier been the case with golf and tennis, these wealthy men provided training facilities for young athletes, establishments where country boys could develop the skill, the power and the devotion that assured the future of skiing.

The very solidity of the new ski areas, with the great steel towers of the lifts anchored in concrete, the motors clicking and the electronic devices buzzing, contributed to the permanence of the sport. There were casualties, of course, and the first of them was the easiness and informality of the old days when everyone climbed. Leisurely conversation vanished in the frantic rush of skiers to cram as many downhill runs as possible into the short winter days. The thrill of accomplishment in having climbed a mountain, accompanied by a long rest on the summit to savor the scenery, disappeared forever from skiing. What the ski lift era did produce, however, was a vast increase in the number of skilled, trained, precise skiers, along with an infinitely better quality of skiing. A lift skier might make twenty long runs in a day on unwearied muscles compared to the two or three runs he could achieve by climbing.

The first and greatest Maecenas was Averell Harriman, in his time a notable polo player, who did not become a skier until he was forty-five. Encouraged by his daughter Kathleen, he made a tour of the European ski resorts, inspected them with a practiced businessman's eye, and remembered that his Union Pacific ran through the Rocky Mountains. He decided to put the railroad's money to work in a manner that would give him his own winter resort while establishing the Union Pacific as the glamorous way to travel West with a stopover in the Rockies for skiing. In the fall of 1935 he hired an Austrian expert, Count Felix von Schaffgotsch, and dispatched him on an inspection tour of the mountains served by the Union Pacific. There were a lot of mountains—the Grand Tetons, the Sawtooth Mountains in Idaho, the Wasatches in Utah, the Sierra Nevada and the great extinct volcanoes extending along the Pacific slope from Mt. Shasta, California, past Mts. Hood and Rainier to Mt. Baker almost on the Canadian border. All had merits and demerits. The Pacific Coast peaks were buried under a tremendous tonnage of snow during a long winter season, but it was heavy, wet snow of almost concrete consistency. For months on end the mountains were under the clouds. The Sierra Nevada had the same disability. The Wasatches were, at the time, remote, and subject to avalanches, but the powder snow that fell on them was, perhaps, the finest in the world. What Schaffgotsch was looking for was deep powder and sunshine too. That combination was what made the Alps so sought after by skiers.

He found the combination at Ketchum, Idaho, a little cow town at the end of a branch line fifty miles north of Shoshone. A luxury train, the Portland Rose, ran through Shoshone from Chicago to Portland, and there were convenient connections from Los Angeles and San Francisco. But from Shoshone to Ketchum, there was only a twice-weekly "mixed" train, a collection of freight cars and one day coach lit by kerosene lamps that swayed up the tracks to their end, in a sunny bowl where bare mountainsides rose up from meadows covered with sagebrush. Averell Harriman arrived in his private car within two weeks, and the saga of Sun Valley began.

It wasn't, in fact, all that classic a saga. The snow season in most years began just before Christmas and ended on the valley floor in early April—hardly comparable to the highest-altitude European resorts. The first year, with dozens present for the grand opening, it didn't snow a flake until New Year's Eve. But it was, indeed, a typically American creation, the first ski resort built totally from scratch, whereas those in Europe started as summer resorts and gravitated later to skiing. It was also a wonderfully beautiful concept. Sun Valley Lodge, constructed of tinted concrete to resemble timber, was as lavish as—and far more modern than—the unmatched Palace Hotel in St. Moritz. The Alpine village that surrounded it could have been transplanted bodily from Switzerland. The mountains were not, perhaps, as steep, but on the east side of Baldy Mountain there were tremendous open snow bowls that certainly equaled the Alpine best. And, indeed, there was the sun.

Probably Harriman's wisest decision was to hire the most effective public relations man in the United States. Steve Hannagan had made Miami Beach famous. He did the same by choosing the name of Sun Valley—a magnetic word to most American skiers who did their skiing in bitter cold weather and generally under gray skies. He flooded the newspapers with photos of men skiing stripped to the waist and girls in bras and shorts. The exaggeration was not too great. In December and January the temperatures stayed around zero, and shirtsleeve skiing was impossible. But in February, the sun beat down on the semiarid hills and all Hannagan's publicity came true. It was the first touch of glamour in a sport that had been considered the private preserve of the muscleman.

Harriman and Hannagan between them attracted a cosmopolitan patronage—Gary Cooper, Claudette Colbert, Norma Shearer and Ann Sothern from Hollywood; Cabots from Boston; members of society from New York, the Midwest and the Pacific Coast; an impressive collection of Austrian ski teachers in the country's largest ski school, and even a gambler or two who set up a casino in nearby Ketchum. When, perhaps due to some gentle prodding, Idaho in 1938 reduced to thirty days the residence requirements for a divorce, Sun Valley became more popular than Reno among the rich who wanted to relax in reticence.

The ski instructors were as glamorous as the patrons. A series of marriages resulted. Hoyt Smith, daughter of a Salt Lake City banker, married Friedl Pfeiffer, later the founder of skiing at Aspen. Sepp Froehlich married Natalie Rogers, of the oil family; Norma Shearer married Marty Arrouge, the son of a Basque sheepherding family, and most of them lived happily ever after. There were, of course, exceptions. For an Austrian peasant boy suddenly elevated to godhood because of his skill on skis, the ambience was a little hectic and the scent of money was overpowering. One teacher married a rich, unfortunate girl who was a hopeless alcoholic. During her rare appearances on the ski hills, she required an instructor on either side to keep her upright.

But along with all this glitter there was Averell Harriman's serious interest in skiing and his concern that the sport should develop. In 1938 he established the Harriman Cup, still one of the premier events of American ski racing. By providing free board and room he encouraged young racers to winter at Sun Valley. Gretchen Fraser, later to win America its first gold medal in a Winter Olympics, was one product refined to champion status by Sun Valley. Barney McLean, a national champion, was another. Sun Valley, in its own way, became the St. Anton of North America—the place where ski teaching, ski racing and skiing for pleasure reached an apogee. When, in 1939, Dick Durrance shot down the Steilhang on the Warm Springs Run, saving himself by inches from a crash into the trees, it also became a historic site among those who respected speed, skill and daring.

Unknown to Harriman, the Midwest was harboring another Maecenas. Fred Pabst, of the brewing family, was determined to dominate the ski lift business. A Dartmouth graduate, in 1935 he visited his alma mater during Winter Carnival and noted with interest the J-bar lift on Oak Hill. "The damn thing was put together with baling wire," Pabst said later. "The motor wasn't right, and the cable kept jumping off the sheaves. I got hold of Gordon Bannerman, chief engineer for the American Steel and Wire Company, and worked with his engineers day and night until we came up with a J-bar that didn't cause trouble." During 1936 and 1937 Pabst installed five J-bars—at Intervale and Plymouth, New Hampshire, at Mt. Aeolus, Vermont, at Lake George, New York, and at Rib Mountain near Wausau, Wisconsin. Just to keep out the competition, he also built rope tows at Houghton and Iron Mountain, Michigan, and at Hill 70 near St. Sauveur, Quebec.

The business for his Michigan and Wisconsin ski areas had to be generated in Chicago and Milwaukee—where, Pabst said, "nobody knew thing one about skiing." He cajoled some of the big department stores into providing a stock of skis and boots that could be rented, but this still left his customers hundreds of miles from the skiing. Pabst found a solution. He chartered whole trains—"bought 'em, you might say, and if I didn't fill 'em

I had to foot the bill." The first train was due to leave Chicago at 6:30 A.M. on a wintry Saturday. Pabst had hired musicians in Tyrolean costumes; the bar and restaurant cars were well stocked, but nobody showed up. Twenty-five minutes later he was almost knocked down and trampled by would-be skiers, who jammed the train to standing room only. The railroad had forgotten that the first commuter trains from the Chicago suburbs didn't start running until six o'clock in the morning. "Those were wild rides," Pabst recalls. "It took about four hours each way to and from Wausau and six and a half hours each way to and from Iron Mountain. The result was, if lucky, you got half a day's skiing. But in those days the sport was so new and the skiers so bad that they got their real fun out of the train ride."

As skiing's first monopolist, Pabst had his troubles. The lifts on Mt. Aeolus and at Lake George seldom had snow. He found himself rushing frantically from Canada to New England to the Midwest. Finally in 1938 he settled on Bromley Mountain, near Manchester, Vermont, as the place he would like to concentrate his efforts. He built a J-bar lift on Little Bromley, a low hill, that turned a 35-degree corner and was the awe of the engineers. Between 1941 and 1943, he gradually pulled out all his scattered J-bars and concentrated them on Bromley. This wasn't always easy. The burghers of Lake George, who had leased land to Pabst for his J-bar, adamantly refused to let him take it away, even though snow conditions were abominable and customers nonexistent. A rancorous lawsuit ensued, and the sales of Pabst Blue Ribbon beer hit a temporary low in Lake George. Pabst, however, finally won, and Lake George's dream of a winter wonderland went glimmering.

The result of concentrating all his lifts on Bromley proved highly satisfactory to Pabst. He had created the biggest, most highly developed, mass ski center in the United States. Pabst, as he describes it, became a snow farmer. He used tractors, hay rakes, and a dozen other rustic devices to keep the snow rolled and packed, to pull it back on the trails after the swing turns of skiers had flung it to the sides, and to break it into crystals when rains and thaws, followed by a freeze, produced an icy cover.

Skiing, which had been a rather orderly sport up to then, became a supermarket, with tremendous waiting lines, teeming crowds, and restaurants equipped to feed 1,500 skiers per hour. Some purists began to refer to Bromley as "Mascara Mountain." By making skiing easy enough for the duffer, Pabst attracted certain citified types whose previous haunts had been Grossinger's and the Concord in the Sullivan County Catskills, kosher resorts of immense repute.

The same thing happened, a year earlier, at North Conway, New Hampshire. Harvey Dow Gibson, the man who brought the Hannes Schneider school to the East, wanted to do something more spectacular for the town in which he had lived as a boy. He called on Pabst to ask his advice. Pabst, who rather fancied the idea of opening another ski center, overwhelmed him with oratory. "After half an hour," recalls Pabst, "he said to me, 'You've convinced me. I'm going to build my own place.'"

Gibson bought all Cranmore Mountain, on the edge of North Conway, ripped out the trees and created two huge open slopes hundreds of feet wide, the biggest then in existence. However, these slopes faced west, toward the prevailing winds. Half a foot of snow might fall during the night but by morning the slopes would be covered with sheet ice. Gibson's manager, Phil Robertson, developed a mat, studded with nails, drawn by a tractor, and known as the Magic Carpet. This would pulverize the ice and provide a passable surface for skiers. However, there were times when even the Magic Carpet was frustrated. One skier still recalls starting a turn on ice at the top of the mountain and being unable to finish it until he reached the bottom, a mile away.

Either Gibson did not know about the newly developed chair lifts, or he didn't like them. He wanted uphill transportation that would operate for sightseers in summer and for skiers in winter. New Englanders are notably inventive, and Robertson came up with the idea of the ski-mobile. Little open cars with rubber tires, rolling on a wooden trestle and attached to an endless cable, carried passengers to the top of Cranmore. It was an ingenious idea for an experimental period, and it really wowed the

Boston trade, only two hours distant by snow train. With a nod toward Averell Harriman, Gibson bought and renovated the gracious old Eastern Slope Inn and made it an annex to his ski business within walking distance of the slopes. The food was good, the wines were excellent, and the orchestra was notable for its ability to play almost any selection a guest might desire.

One night in 1940, after Germany and England had gone to war, the orchestra enjoyed its most severe test and came through with flying violin bows. The German consul-general from New York had come up to ski with a group of friends from the consulate. Seated at one table nearby was Hannes Schneider, whom the consul's supreme leader had destined for a concentration camp. Seated at another, with friends, was Mrs. Gibson. She beckoned the orchestra leader to her side. "Don't play anything that doesn't have music or lyrics by a German Jew," she whispered. The orchestra responded with Mendelssohn by the bucketful, Heine's "Die Lorelei," "Wien, Wien, Nur Du Allein," and half a dozen others by authors or composers with impeccably non-Aryan backgrounds. The consul, with red slowly creeping up his neck, stuck it out for a dignified length of time but finally stalked out with his covey of Nazis. After that, the orchestra was permitted by Mrs. Gibson to play a few Aryan tunes.

What North Conway may have lacked in chichi—the Gibsons were not much for show—it made up through the august presence of Schneider. Morning at the ski school was a sight not to be forgotten. Apprehensive students lined up to be assigned to classes by the great Hannes, and these assignments were not to be argued with. Brash skiers who professed a greater knowledge than they had might last a few moments in, say, the advanced stem-christiania class, but then the shadow of Hannes would fall over the proceedings, and they would be dispatched tactfully to a lower group to learn the basics better. One student estimated he made a thousand stem turns before Hannes, in a murmured colloquy, motioned him on to nirvana in the next highest class. Learning at North Conway was a grave and mannered business, something like a performance of *Parsifal* during Holy Week. Those who learned from Schneider never forgot what he taught them—an embarrassment these days because the technique has changed. Even the New England boys who joined his ski school developed an Austrian accent. Cries of "Mo-ah schulter! Mo-ah schulter!" ("More shoulder! More shoulder!") rang across the Cranmore Mountain slopes.

Once solid men such as Harriman, Pabst and Gibson had shown the way, the patrons of skiing came thick and fast, even including government. The state of New Hampshire in 1938 constructed the first aerial tramway in North America on Cannon Mountain, site of the Old Man of the Mountain. Cannon was the product of Alexander H. Bright, a distinguished Boston ski racer who had traveled often on such conveyances in the Alps. Somehow he generated so much enthusiasm that the frugal citizens voted a bond issue, and the tramway became one of the big drawing cards of eastern skiing. It was a tremendous attraction in summer, earning enough from sightseers to pay the winter losses. In winter it had its drawbacks. On very windy days, the twin cabins attached to the cable—one ascending as the other descended—would sway so much they couldn't get past the towers without getting caught in them. Occasionally skiers would be hung up for half an hour or even longer while the cabins inched up to the towers, an attendant stuck his foot out, and the cabins were guided past the steel framework.

The same year, in the middle of a huge public works program, Secretary of the Interior Ickes, head of the Public Works Administration, was persuaded to build a $3,000,000 luxury lodge at Timberline on Mt. Hood, Oregon. Timberline Lodge brought a new dimension of luxury to the Far West where, to say the least, accommodations had been primitive. Huge logs arched over a tremendous lobby; the curtains were handmade and the hardware hand-hammered, and every room had its own bath. A mile-long chair lift extended from the lodge onto the open upper slopes of Hood. The only problem was that the snow fell so fast, so thickly and so heavily that on occasion the lift had to be dug out before it could operate, and on one occasion was almost completely buried. Yet the result was to establish skiing impregnably in the Pacific Northwest.

On the East Coast, a New York newspaperman and skier named Hal Burton decided that the Lake Placid, New York, area needed a ski lift to round out the facilities built for the 1932 Winter Olympics. The difficulty was that the nearest suitable mountain, Whiteface, was part of the state-owned Adirondack Forest Preserve, to remain, by constitutional provision, "forever as wild forest land." However, I knew Walter Brown, secretary to Governor Herbert H. Lehman. Through Brown I secured an appointment, stated my case with all the passion at my command, and was preparing to leave because the governor had made no comment. "Well, I think I agree," Lehman finally said mildly. "I don't ski but I have some nephews and nieces who do, and they say it's great." The governor endorsed a proposed constitutional amendment which sailed through two successive legislatures and then was submitted to the voters on November 7, 1941. Against the bitter opposition of conservationists and most newspapers, the amendment was approved by exactly 9,000 votes out of approximately 2,000,000. *The New Yorker,* in its "Talk of the Town," devoted some space to the phenomenon of the only state constitution in which the word skiing is used. World War II intervened, however, and Whiteface was not completed until 1957 when, by coincidence, Averell Harriman was governor of New York State.

Private entrepreneurs were just as busy as government agencies during this time. Janet and Bradford Mead, of a well-to-do Rutland, Vermont, family, imported the first T-bar lift from Switzerland in 1938 and set it up on Pico Peak, between Rutland and Woodstock. Pico, as the skiers knew it, was a great sensation because of its nearly vertical "A" slope, an ultrachallenging little hill. It was also the easiest lift center to reach from New York, served both by overnight snow trains to Rutland and by an adequate highway net. Such durable young racers as Wendy Cram, only five feet two inches tall, learned the fine points of slalom at Pico and went on to national importance. More important for the growth of skiing, the New York City clubs held intramural races here that spread the gospel of downhill and slalom racing as a way of life that transcended mere turning on a slope.

There was a genuine "Pico mystique," nurtured by the hospitality and originality of the Meads. Their daughter Andrea, helped along by fine instruction from the resident Swiss ski teacher, Karl Acker, went on to win America's only double victory in the 1950 Oslo Winter Olympics—two gold medals for slalom and giant slalom.

The Maecenean apogee came on both coasts in 1939. Walt Disney, the movie producer, sponsored the western development; Joseph B. ("Joe") Ryan, son of the financier Thomas Fortune Ryan, was responsible for what happened in the East. Disney, a new hand at skiing, came in somewhat by happenstance. San Francisco skiers were searching for a place in the Sierra Nevada where something bigger than a rope tow could be built. The prime explorers were Hannes Schroll, a cheerful Austrian who used to leap and yodel his way down the western racecourses, and John Wiley, born in England but long a San Franciscan. After long hours of trudging about the Sierra Nevada on skis they discovered a peak called Mt. Lincoln, not far off the Southern Pacific Railroad and the main highway to the east over Donner Pass. Disney showed so much enthusiasm and invested so heavily, a mountain was named after him, and the first chair lift in California ran up it. The trouble in getting to Sugar Bowl, as the area was called, was the deep snow. Visitors were loaded into sleds behind huge tractors and bucked and lurched their way into the charmed valley. It became, all too quickly, the "in" place for moneyed San Francisco residents, a type of "society" ski area. It was also the first designed for people who built their own ski lodges, which automatically made it exclusive. There was a lodge with limited capacity, but guests of members generally kept it full.

That same year Joe Ryan burst upon the scene in the Canadian Laurentians—the most fiery, imaginative and moody man ever to create a ski area. Ryan had climbed a ski trail on Mt. Tremblant two years earlier in the company of his friend, Lowell Thomas. "Too damn much work," he concluded after floundering in the deep snow for hours. "Maybe I'll do something about it." Indeed he did do something. After two years of negotiating with the Quebec government, he bought much of the highest peak in the Laurentians and spent more than $2,000,000 creating a uniquely attractive area. The first chair lift in Canada ran up the southern slopes of the mountain, directly over a weird-looking trail known as the Flying Mile. This trail came down over a whole series of ledges from twenty to fifty feet high. Rather than blow them out at prohibitive cost, Ryan devised a series of wooden aprons that were attached to the cliffs, held the snow, and permitted a descent a little short of suicidal.

At the base of the mountain, along the shores of Lac Tremblant, he built a charming French Canadian village, in the Norman style of the early *habitants,* and a chapel copied from the Ile d'Orleans, on the St. Lawrence River below Quebec City. It was very definitely Joe Ryan's feudal fief. A Philadelphia Mainliner from St. David's, he drew in many of his friends from New York and Philadelphia. The lodge was ostensibly public, but in fact Ryan vetted just about every guest. If, by mischance, an individual or a group didn't measure up to his standards—and these could vary from initial enthusiasm to undying hatred—he simply ordered the unfortunate wayfarers to leave, sometimes in the middle of the night.

Though Ryan made an infinitesimal number of exceptions, his general attitude toward Jews as guests was somewhat similar to that of Hitler before *Kristallnacht.* He did not want them; he refused to have them; and if by chance an unforwarned Jew wandered innocently in, he was expelled amid a torrent of invective from the proprietor. Early in World War II one of the Barons de Rothschild, a fugitive from overrun France, appeared in the lobby with friends and not unnaturally signed his name to a registration card. "No, no, NO!" roared Ryan when apprised of the visitation. Advancing on the puzzled Baron, he bellowed, "Out!" and pointed to the door like God expelling Adam and Eve from the Garden of Eden.

"But I like eet here," expostulated the Baron as he was propelled through the door.

When friends pointed out that a Rothschild from France was scarcely a Ginsberg from Brooklyn, Ryan's succinct reply was,

"Who gives a damn?" His attitude was extreme, it wounded a good many people, and it embarrassed many of his friends, but that social anti-Semitism was commonplace in most summer and winter resorts before World War II, as common then as it is rare now. Some of the most humble as well as all of the most elegant ski resorts, when advertising in *The New York Times,* included as a matter of course the phrase "Gentiles only" or "restricted clientele." After a certain amount of public protest, this later gave way to "churches nearby," and one ingenious ski lodge at Lake Placid employed a punishingly oblique sentence, "Guests will enjoy our Christian religious library." Jews nevertheless did ski, along with everyone else, and provided a leaven all the way from the Amateur Ski Club of New York to the elbowing crowds on the snow trains.

Ryan, it must be added in justice, was capable of counter-balancing his reservoirs of rage with great moments of sweetness. He spent tens of thousands of dollars encouraging impecunious young racers to come to Tremblant, and provided free skiing and equipment for the penniless youngsters from the barren habitant farms. He literally invested himself in the mountain, along with too much of his fortune. He had developed lifts on the north as well as the south side of the mountain, but there was no descent road from one side to another. He spent a fortune building a broad, paved highway to link the two areas. These, with the other punishing costs of operating a ski area, made a worrisome burden. One day in the later 1940s he fell to his death from a New York hotel window. Even those who found him most difficult as friend or boniface acknowledge now the tremendous lift he gave to skiing.

The ultimate Maecenas of the prewar period probably invested the least cash money of any in his group, but gave more shape and form to American skiing than any other individual. Roland Palmedo, a New York investment banker, had founded the Williams Outing Club when an undergraduate in 1915, founded the Amateur Ski Club in 1931, and pursued a relentless search for good places to ski in the East. Piloting his own plane, he would fly over the New England mountains in the spring to see where the snow stayed longest and where ski centers might possibly be developed. This in due course led him to Stowe, where he climbed the old carriage road to the summit ridge of the mountain and found phenomenal depths of snow. With the help of interested local men, he pushed for the development of a more adequate trail system and, once it was under way, helped to provide discreet inspiration by appearing with cases of beer for the sweaty woodcutters. Trail clearing wasn't mechanized in those days. Men with huge buck saws had to fell the big trees, saw them into manageable lengths, and roll them off into the woods. Stumps had to be sawed as close as possible to the ground. The whole process hadn't changed much since the 1880s.

Stowe could have puttered along for years as a mildly popular, pleasant little place in a remote corner of the Green Mountains if Palmedo had not taken action. He enlisted a group of friends, among them Thomas and Godfrey Rockefeller, and raised $75,000 to establish the Mt. Mansfield Lift Company. This corporation built the first chair lift in the East, which opened in 1939. The combination of good snow, not too much wind, and a classic New England setting immediately made Stowe *the* place to ski. This did not, however, make Stowe an earthly paradise. Those who have the creativity to conceive of great ski developments are first dismissed as visionary and then criticized when they succeed. Two founding members of the Mt. Mansfield Ski Club, whose formation was encouraged by Palmedo, had to be pulled apart at one meeting to stop a fist fight. A young man named George Morrell, operator of the only hotel on the mountain, the Lodge, brooded his way into a feud with Palmedo, and as the resort prospered Stowe grew more, rather than less, rancorous. Palmedo in fact was the community's greatest benefactor. He set the tone for a resort that, despite overcrowding at times, maintains its elegance today along with a solid devotion to the basics of skiing.

4

Quite by Accident

AMONG ALL THE FRACTURES of the tibia or fibia, comminuted, compound or spiral, only one was destined to have a permanent effect on American skiing. The victim was a Greenwich, Connecticut, insurance broker named Charles Minot Dole, who—at the moment of truth—was totally unaware that he had just tumbled into history but acutely aware, as he put it later, that his right ankle was "hurting one hell of a lot." Dole, up to that point, had been anonymous but passionate in his pursuit of opportunities to ski. He had taken up the sport at Lake Placid Club in 1933, had joined the Amateur Ski Club, and had fallen victim to a compulsion to ski anywhere in the East anytime there was snow. This compulsion had carried him from Placid to Peckett's, then the reigning debutante among eastern ski resorts, and had introduced him to the secrets of the Arlberg technique. Previously, his skiing repertoire had been based largely on the controlled fall, meaning that he simply sat back and let the snows enfold him whenever his speed downhill became too much to manage. Occasionally, he essayed the Norwegian telemark, still the most elegant and often the most awkward of skiing turns. This maneuver, intended for snows of a depth rarely found in the East, involved the shoving forward of one ski. The tip of the rearmost ski was then placed delicately against the midpoint of the extended ski, which resulted in a long, sweeping turn calculated to induce a double hernia in all but Norwegians, who grew up with it.

Dole recalls that skiing at Peckett's was hail fellow, well met only on the slopes. Katherine Peckett was all-out in her enthusiasm, but her father entertained some doubts about people who chose to stay with him during the coldest, most bone-chilling time of the year and positively reveled in their misery. Peckett *père* took pride in his brightly waxed floors, and was not about to permit them to be marred by heavy ski boots. As a result, all guests humbly took off their boots before entering and padded about in stocking feet or slippers, much as in a Japanese home. Despite this rather frosty Yankee caveat against blitheness of spirit, Peckett's engendered its own intimate little group, of which Dole and his wife, Jane, were, so to speak, charter members. Their interest in skiing led them to Stowe for a New Year's 1936 holiday in company with their friends Frank and Jean Edson, neighbors in Greenwich. Although a fine rain was falling when they arrived, they decided to take a few runs on a slope near the Lodge, the only inn on the mountain. Dole, wearing the rigid cable bindings of the era, took a fall and sprained his right ankle. After he had soaked it in hot water and wrapped it in an ace bandage, it seemed better.

The next morning the Doles and Edsons started up the Toll Road again. It was one of those grim January days when the trees stand black against the dull sheen of rain-soaked snow and the mountain peaks are enveloped in a bluish haze. The drizzle changed to rain, and the party decided against climbing to the top. The snow, which had been reasonably fast and easy to ski on, changed with rising temperatures to a sticky, tricky, soggy mess. Pushing off boldly, Dole attempted a stem christiania on his weak ankle, which gave way halfway through the turn. He took what skiers describe as an "eggbeater," tumbling forward over the skis and then coming to a jolting stop as his ski tips broke through the snow. He heard no snapping sound, but it was obvious to him that his right ankle was not in the position an ankle ought to be in. He went into shock, the invariable aftermath of a broken bone. Edson stayed with him and took off his own parka to cover the shivering Dole. The two wives skied to the base of the mountain for help. The first person they met was a local boy, the ski instructor, whose kindly comment was: "Anybody fool enough to hurt himself on this dumb trail deserves what he gets." And that was the last they saw of him.

The desperate wives finally rounded up two other skiers. The four of them seized a piece of corrugated tin roofing lying alongside the Toll House woodpile and dragged it to the supine Dole. The tin was so short that Dole could rest only his injured leg on it; his buttocks dragged in the snow as he was hauled down to the main highway. Driven ten miles to the nearest doctor, he received the cheery advice that the break was too complicated to be set by anyone but a specialist. With his leg in a temporary aluminum splint, Dole returned to the Lodge. By this time the ankle hurt so much that Dole knew he could not possibly bear the cramped auto ride back to New York, nearly nine hours over winding, bumpy roads. He would have to take the train, which left nearby Waterbury, Vermont, at midnight. With the help of a bottle of Scotch and some codeine, he lasted until his wife and friends could deposit him in a berth aboard the Central Vermont Railroad's "Washingtonian." This by good luck stopped en route at Greenwich, but the ride was scarcely smooth. Dole's doctor set the ankle, but he was on crutches for months after the accident. During this period of convalescence he had plenty of time for reflection. One of the thoughts that repeatedly crossed his mind was that there must be some better way to care for skiers injured on a mountainside.

As a matter of fact, the first beginnings of a better way were already in gestation. Roland Palmedo had skied frequently at Davos, in the Swiss Grisons, where the community maintained the Parsenn Patrol. This organization of rescue workers, who collected a fee for hauling the injured off the slopes, was highly trained in first aid. Thus simple fractures did not become compound through rough handling, and more complicated injuries were cared for in a fashion that would not make them worse. The year Dole broke his ankle, Palmedo had encouraged the ski clubs at Stowe, Burlington, Vermont, Pittsfield, Massachusetts,

and Lake Placid to organize ski patrols. These informal organizations had no specifically defined mission. If, in the course of a
day's skiing, patrolmen came across an accident, it was their job
to locate a toboggan and to help take the injured person off the
mountain. Local doctors and Red Cross chapters furnished the
rudiments of first aid training; at the time there was no formulated doctrine dealing with skiing injuries or the problems
created by subzero temperatures. Quite independently, a patrol
also was organized by Portland, Oregon, skiers to serve the high
slopes of Mt. Hood. This patrol was patterned after the efficient
Bergwacht, the mountain rescue organization developed in Germany and Austria. Because Hood is heavily used by inexperienced mountain climbers, the patrol was busier in the summer
than it was in the winter.

Those early patrols undertook some grueling missions. At Lake
Placid, just after Hitler overran Norway, a Norwegian seaman
disappeared from his hotel one day. He wasn't back by dark, so
in the middle of the night when the temperature was 20 below
zero, the ski patrol set out to track him. His footmarks led them
on a wildly erratic course, many miles long, until at daybreak
they found his body. He had committed suicide. The Stowe
patrol in 1937 manned the Nose Dive one day when the snow
was sheer ice and a blanket of dense fog surged around the
mountain. At each steep pitch, where racers might get into
trouble, a patrolman was stationed with a red flag. As he heard
the clatter of steel edges through the murk, he would wave his
flag frantically. Invariably the racer fell, and slid down cursing
to the bottom of the pitch before he could regain his feet. The
speeds achieved in that race, the Vermont Downhill Champion-
ship, were something less than sensational. But thanks to the
shivering patrolmen with their red flags, not one skier was injured and the race did not have to be called because of fog.

It took the death of his best friend to move Dole one ski
length closer to history. In late February 1937, Frank Edson
stopped by to announce that he planned to race for the Amateur
Ski Club in the New York interclub championships at Pittsfield
(Massachusetts) State Forest. The name of the racing trail was

prophetic, the Ghost Trail. "Frank," said Dole earnestly, "I think you're making a mistake. You can't ski much better than I do, and you'll be racing over your head." Edson—tall, blond, well-muscled—shrugged and went his way. The races were held on a Saturday. When, by Sunday night, Dole had not heard from Edson, he rang the latter's home. A weeping maid answered the phone. "Mr. Frank's broke both his legs and both his arms," she said. "He's in the hospital in Pittsfield." Dole hung up, paused a minute, and reached for the phone just as it rang. The message was chilling. Edson was dead. He had run into a tree, breaking three ribs. The shattered ends had penetrated his lungs, and he died from internal bleeding. The Pittsfield patrol, untrained in so exotic an injury, had done its best. He had been evacuated within minutes. Even today, when ski patrolmen are so highly trained, it is doubtful his life could have been saved. Another racer named Duncan Read, injured the same day, never will forget the occasion. "I can remember seeing Frank Edson's casket being put into the baggage car as the stretcher with me on it was taken into a drawing room on the same train," he recalls.

This was not the first American skiing fatality, but it was a numbing shock to Edson's friends in the Amateur Ski Club. A special meeting was called at once to discuss what could be done to prevent similar tragedies. It was obvious that the old, fatalistic days and the old, fatalistic attitudes no longer were relevant to a sport in which speed had taken the place of leisurely puttering.

Palmedo summed up the situation. "The time has come," he said, "for a general study of safety in skiing, and it is up to this club to undertake it." Turning to Dole, he said, "Minnie, you were Frank's best friend. Will you be chairman of a special study committee?"

Dole accepted the appointment, and Palmedo named John E. P. Morgan and Borden Helmer to work with him. The new committee sent out hundreds of questionnaires to local ski clubs, asking them to report all accidents and to explain how they were handled. To Dole's disappointment, only about a hundred answers came in, and of those who answered less than half were

willing to cooperate. The rest of the responders were either indifferent or hostile. One reply from the Boston area accused the
committee members of being "sissies, spoilsports, and frighteners
of mothers." Others, from the owners of ski resorts or lodges, expressed the fear that an open discussion of skiing accidents
would drive newcomers away from the sport.

Boston, seat of the most opposition, had over the years bred
some ultratough skiers. The nearby White Mountains were
rough, rocky, windy and cold; skiing in the area had developed
from the early mountain climbers of the Appalachian Mountain
Club and Harvard Mountaineering Club. They were contemptu-
ous of gadgets and indifferent to personal comfort. Skiing, to
them, was in the main an invitation to do battle with the elements: the worse the day, the greater the challenge. A "what the
hell!" attitude was accurately reflected in the name given one of
the early ski clubs in the area, the Black and Blue Trail Smashers.

Dole, after inquiry, established that the bellwether club was
the Ski Club Hochgebirge of Boston. He knew none of the members, but he did establish that two of the most prominent were
ski racers, Alec Bright and Robert L. Livermore. To Dole's surprise, Bright promised to help "in any way I can." Livermore
busied himself with missionary work, and, after some grumbling,
the Boston area clubs cooperated in organizing a ski patrol. The
good work was helped along by an inspiration of John E. P.
Morgan. He suggested, though the idea seems odd in retrospect, that interest in skiing safety might be increased through
the creation of a Broken Bone Club. Anyone sending $1.50 to
Dole was given a small silver pin in the design of a fractured leg
bone. One of the first members was Alec Bright. Nobody was
better qualified to talk about fractures. He had fractured both
legs six separate times while skiing faster than anyone around,
most of the accidents occurring after he had passed age forty.

The concept of national status for the patrol developed in
1938 when the National Downhill Championships were held at
Stowe. At the request of the Mt. Mansfield Ski Club, Dole took
charge of safety arrangements. Toboggans were cached at intervals along the Nose Dive. Beside each toboggan stood a pa-

trolman, in sight of the man above and below him. If an injury occurred at any point, all patrolmen above that point would move up one station, and the vacant spot at the bottom would be filled in by a standby. Perhaps, the sight of all that massed first aid gave the racers pause, or perhaps it was luck, but only one skier was injured, and he managed to make the finish line under his own power.

Present for the occasion was Roger Langley, president of the National Ski Association. Langley, a chubby schoolmaster from Barre, Massachusetts, was an indifferent skier, but he toiled up the trail to join Dole high on the mountain. A keening wind swept clouds of snow across the Nose Dive, and the two men resorted to a special sort of first aid, a bottle of Vat 69. Between occasional sips of Scotch, Langley expressed his admiration for Dole's arrangements. "This patrol you put together today is terrific," he said. "What a wonderful thing it would be for skiing if we could organize patrols on a national basis. If I appointed you chairman of a national ski patrol committee, would you take the job?"

"I'd sure as hell try," said Dole, and the deal was sealed with another nip. When he got back to Greenwich, he sat down at his portable typewriter with a list of ski clubs belonging to the National Ski Association and fired off the first of some 35,000 letters. He wrote most of these, and dictated many more, before he finally retired as director of the National Ski Patrol in 1950.

Patrols soon were organized wherever there was snow. The Red Cross cooperated. One of its subofficers, Dr. L. M. Thompson, was named the first medical director of the National Ski Patrol System (NSPS). He formulated accident report cards to be filled in by patrolmen and wrote the original Red Cross *Winter First Aid Manual,* published late in 1938. This book exploded a number of folk myths about how to care for the injured in cold weather. Liquor, a favorite remedy, was outlawed: The first warmth engendered by a slug of whiskey simply led to a greater chill thereafter. Frostbitten spots used to be rubbed with snow, which led to chilblains or damage to the skin. Patrolmen were directed to bring frostbite victims into a warm room and to let them thaw out slowly. Injured persons were not to be moved from where they fell except by patrolmen; amateurs in first aid might compound a simple fracture or, in the case of back injuries, cause the severing of the spinal cord. Special, light-weight splints were developed, and prospective patrolmen were required to take thirty hours of Red Cross winter first aid train-ing before being accepted by the NSPS.

Among the aspirants who took this course was Alec Bright. He viewed his training seriously. At one session, Bright was asked to demonstrate the points where pressure should be applied to stop bleeding on the head and neck. Bright applied pressure with a vengeance, to the point where the volunteer serving as his patient complained of faintness. Released from Bright's iron grip he stepped outside, fell down and broke his leg. The first aid class had its first opportunity to demonstrate the technique of applying traction to a leg (pulling the broken parts apart so they could slide back to fit together) and then putting on a traction splint to hold the broken leg immobile. Bright liked to travel so fast and to ski the mountain so often that he was not, initially, regarded as a prime prospect for a national patrolman. He agreed only on one condition: twice a day he would be allowed to take off his patrol insignia and to run the trails as fast as he wished.

Dole's own first aid instructor was Dr. Whitman Reynolds, a Greenwich neighbor, later to become the national medical di-rector of the NSPS. Reynolds, a rather retiring chap, was ex-plaining to a class of prospective patrolmen one night how to use chemical heating pads, which needed to be dampened in order to function.

One of the women in the class asked him, "What should I do if there isn't any water?"

Reynolds smiled. "Well," he said, "if you haven't got a match to melt some snow, and if there isn't a nearby brook, I'll give you three guesses . . ." He paused, shrugged his shoulders and dropped the subject, amid laughter.

Dole himself had not been a national patrolman very long be-fore he was confronted by his first accident case—his wife, Jane.

The Doles were skiing on a hill at the Greenwich Country Club when Mrs. Dole fell and injured her knee. Dole knelt beside her and realized that the knee bone was displaced. Traction was the answer. He took her heel in his hands and tugged. There was a snapping sound, and she sighed with relief. He carried her to the car and took her to the hospital, where the doctor said it was the first dislocated patella he ever had seen.

By this time, the winter of 1939, reports were pouring in from national patrolmen all over the country. A typical one came in from Stuart Gillespie, of the Metropolitan New York Patrol:

"Complying with your request, my services as a national patrolman were accepted five times. A broken left leg on Hill 70, St.-Sauveur, on February 18. On Easter Sunday I splinted the leg of a Boston girl, skiing for the first time at Intervale, New Hampshire. Next day, I strapped a dislocated knee on the Sherburne Trail. The following Monday, I applied a traction splint on a broken leg on the Taft Trail, and that afternoon I strapped a dislocated shoulder on the Cannon Mt. Trail with the aid of state foresters."

Warren Spacey, working as a section chief at Mt. Waterman, California, reported:

"We found a girl lying at the base of a tree. She was a first aid instructor who had sense enough to permit no one to touch her until experienced help appeared. Our medical adviser soon arrived and told us to get her to a hospital immediately. We got a station wagon and—here is the important part—managed to get her on a litter in *exactly* the position we found her. If we had attempted to straighten her out we would have killed her. She's up now, though her lung is still draining."

A patrolman at Pulaski, New York, had a more complicated job of logistics:

"A skier had suffered ruptured stomach ulcers which required immediate hospital attention. The doctor had called in a plane equipped with skis, which was to fly to an airport four miles east of this village, pick up the patient, and return to a hospital at Syracuse. It was storming so hard the roads were almost impassable, but our job was to get the patient from the ambulance and into the plane. A snowplow preceded a state police car and ambulance and we eventually got within three hundred yards of the airport. A flare path was laid out, and the plane landed at 1:10 A.M. The snow was four feet deep, and a path had to be beaten for the plane before take-off might be possible.

"Five attempts to take off were made without success. Then word came that a locomotive had been found in the Richland railroad yard. We took the patient from the plane to the locomotive. At 3:40 A.M., the engine started for Watertown with the patient and doctor. At 4:55 A.M., a successful operation was finally performed in the hospital."

The most astonishing patrol action involving a plane occurred in the Cascade Mountains of Washington. A Navy bomber, trying to land after a patrol mission, crashed on a remote mountain. Word came to Ome Daiber, a distinguished mountaineer and a member of the patrol. It took Daiber and a team of six other patrolmen two days to reach the plane, miles from the nearest highway, surrounded by avalanche slopes. The Navy had reported five live bombs aboard, fused for dropping. Daiber left his men a safe distance away, scrambled down to the plane, and deactivated the bombs. He really didn't need to, for the crew of three men were dead. The full patrol loaded the bodies on toboggans, dragged them for miles through neck-deep snow, and helped bring them back to the base for burial.

Later in the war, national ski patrolmen demonstrated once more their uncanny ability to pinpoint accidents, however remote from civilization they might take place. Ed Taylor, in time to become Dole's successor as head of the patrol, advised Dole that the Air Force—training pilots at Lowry Field, Denver—was losing more men in crashes than might have been lost in combat. Dole, who was visiting him, agreed it might be a good idea to have the patrol go after downed planes in the mountains and to bring back pilots who had survived or managed to parachute to safety. The commander at Lowry Field concurred. He sent out a plane with a 200-foot orange streamer, supposed to represent a downed plane. The streamer landed high on a peak to the west of Denver. The Denver patrol was given its general location. The members started off on skis, retrieved the streamer, and within 24 hours placed it on the general's desk.

This led, in due course, to Operation May Day, coordinating twenty-four patrols from San Diego, California, to Port Angeles, Washington, in search and rescue work for the Fourth Air Force. Whenever a plane went down, all patrols in the area were notified and the patrol closest to the accident went to the rescue. Patrolmen carried special clearance cards, for equipment aboard Air Force planes was classified. A Portland, Oregon, manufacturer of ski clothing designed a special, rust-colored parka that was to be used exclusively by NSPS members. Other manufacturers agreed not to duplicate the color. It is still a familiar sight at every major American ski area.

This broadening activity cost money, of course. It took some fantastic juggling by Dole to keep the patrol afloat. Patrolmen paid for their own parkas and the first aid belts they wore around their waist; patrols paid for toboggans and splints. But mailing expenses were heavy. At one point Dole borrowed $100 from Godfrey Rockefeller, a devoted skier. When this ran out his associate John Morgan borrowed $200 from a friend, repaying Rockefeller. A complex system of loans developed, but soon this was not enough. The week of February 12, 1940, was designated National Ski Patrol Week. Ski areas provided tin cans into which money could be dropped. Later, Alec Bright conceived the idea of "a nickel a night," a variation of the *kurtax* charged by Swiss resorts to help in financing skiing activities. Local inns kicked in with a nickel per guest per night, and a substantial sum was raised.

One girl, Dole recalls, was approached as she started up the lift at Big Bromley. She refused to contribute. A few hours later she was brought in to the first aid room with a fractured right leg. In tears, she handed over a dollar. "Swampy" Paris, who ran the ski patrol at Tuckerman Ravine, staged five rescues in a day. Dog-tired, he asked his last passenger, a girl with a sprained ankle who complained all the way down about the bumpy ride, for a contribution to the NSPS. "Contribution!" she snarled. "I didn't come up here to pay for a lousy toboggan ride."

5

Pursuit of the Impossible

FEBRUARY 1940 was a raw month in the Green Mountains. Keening winds whipped the powder snow from the summits, and stirred up little whirlwinds in the forests below. It was a physical struggle to climb the ski trails, swept as they were by gales that came straight from the Arctic Circle. It was also a time, as is so often the case during eastern winters, when dusk is greeted with relief—time to sit by a log fire carrying on its own private conversation, and to drown it out with skiers' talk.

At Bromley Mountain, as everywhere skiers gathered that winter, the discussion inevitably came around to the Russo-Finnish War. At Johnny Seesaw's, the oldest ski lodge in the Manchester area, the four men warming their shanks before the fire shared a special interest in that war on skis. Livermore, Langley, Dole and Bright: as much as anyone, they qualified as founders of down-mountain skiing in the United States. Livermore had raced with the American team in the 1936 Olympics; Langley was president of the National Ski Association; Dole had founded the National Ski Patrol; Bright, by then well into his forties, was the dean of American downhill racers.

Pearl Harbor day was nearly two years distant. The strategists in Washington already were considering probable Japanese intentions, but most Americans, if thinking at all of war, thought in terms of an attack by Germany on the continental United States. The fireplace conversation at Johnny Seesaw's got down to the specifics. Livermore, Langley, Dole and Bright were worrying about a winter invasion and an America helpless against troops trained in winter warfare.

"If foreign troops should attack our northeast coast in winter," asked Dole, "can you imagine our Army trying to fight through the sort of weather that's outside tonight? They'd have a hard enough time getting up the roads, let alone trying to branch into the woods and mountains. And if they came down from Montreal along the Champlain Valley, as they might well do, we'd have no soldiers to protect our flanks in the Green Mountains and the Adirondacks." It wasn't so far-fetched an idea. Men on snowshoes fought up and down Lake Champlain during the French and Indian Wars and, later, the Revolutionary War. The Champlain Valley is a classic invasion route, an open plain flanked by mountains that leads directly to the Hudson River at Albany. Once at Albany, a quick enemy thrust down the Hudson to New York would sever the Northeast from the rest of the United States.

"Seems to me," drawled Langley, puffing his pipe, "that I ought to write the Secretary of War and offer him the services of the National Ski Association." The Secretary of War at the time was Harry H. Woodring. Langley didn't know him, but he could see no harm in trying to get through to him.

Langley didn't know it, but the War Department, in its ponderous fashion, was already thinking along somewhat the same lines. On January 6, 1940, the Assistant Secretary of War, Louis A. Johnson, asked General George C. Marshall, Chief of Staff, what consideration had been given to special clothing, equipment, food, transportation and other essentials necessary to an effective field force under winter conditions approximating those of Finland and northern Russia.

Marshall replied three weeks later that winter training had been conducted in Alaska and had been especially successful at Fort Snelling in Minnesota. "It is my intention," he wrote Johnson, "to continue accelerating, where practicable, tests of food, clothing, equipment and transportation in order to standardize for the purpose the types best suited to operations under severe winter conditions." The trouble was, Marshall said, there was no money to undertake large-scale winter maneuvers. He might have added that his first and worst problem was to turn reserve and National Guard officers and enlisted men, as well as draftees, into soldiers; specialized training had to wait a bit.

The low priority given winter troops was apparent when Langley received a frosty answer to his letter to Woodring. The response arrived in late spring. It was the standard brushoff letter, signed by an underling: "The Secretary of War has instructed me to thank you. . . . We will take your offer under consideration."

This wasn't the sort of answer to satisfy Dole. He was an imperious man accustomed to getting what he wanted, not easily discouraged by an official brushoff. He had always led a well-upholstered life. His father, Charles T. Dole, was an officer of the Champion International Paper Company, which supplied coated paper to the *National Geographic* and other magazines. The family, prosperous and well-connected, lived in a roomy Colonial house in Andover, Massachusetts, outside Boston. The younger Dole as a matter of course was sent to Phillips Academy at Andover. He was seventeen and in the fifth form, when the United States entered World War I in 1917. He promptly asked his father if he could have a piece of the action. The answer was a flat "no," so he ignored it to join a volunteer ambulance unit of Andover students.

"We were at the railroad station," Dole recalls, "getting ready to entrain for New York and overseas, but Father had found out about it. He took me by the nape of the neck and pulled me right out. The unit went without me, and I was heartbroken. The boys I had known drove ambulances and saved lives while I had to study." He didn't permit his father's rebuff to discourage him. An ROTC unit was organized at Andover. He joined, and became a captain—"sick with frustration" at the battle stories drifting back from his former classmates in France. But there was light on the horizon. In 1918, on April 18, Dole would become eighteen, able to enlist in the armed services without parental consent. That day he went to his father, who could be forbidding, and said:

"Sir, I am eighteen years old and now I can do what I want to, can't I?"

The senior Dole said, "Well, what do you want to do?"

His son replied, "I want to enlist."

"What for?"

"Because I want to."

Orders to report to the Officers' Training School at Fort Lee, Virginia, came through in October. Dole was to present himself on November 11. He arrived amid the screaming of sirens and the cheering of would-be officers who didn't much want to go to war. It was Armistice Day; the war was over and he was out of it. Dole asked to be taken into training anyway. All he got out of it was the nickname that has stuck with him the rest of his life. A drill sergeant asked him his name one day.

"Charles Minot [pronounced Mye-not] Dole, sir," he replied.

"That's too big a mouthful," said the sergeant. "From now on, we're going to make it Minnie."

As "Minnie," his friends have known him ever since.

The nickname came back to Andover with him in the spring of 1919 when he returned to finish his final year, and it stayed with him when he went on to Yale. A fine tenor, he joined the glee club and in his sophomore year became a member of the Whiffenpoofs, the best college singing group in the country. When he graduated in 1923 he dutifully went to work for a wool company in Lawrence, Massachusetts, as a wool sorter, a traditional starting place for a young man whose family intended him to arrive at the top in business. This, for a high-spirited young man, was Dullsville, in spades, and Dole marvels that he stood it for three years. Rescue came unexpectedly. A young and rich Princeton friend, Bill Brown, came along with a staggering offer of $4,800 a year if Dole would join him in a series of European business ventures. Arriving with Brown in Paris, he was trundled off to the apartment of Brown's lawyer, to be greeted by a lineup of fifty filled martini glasses on the mantelpiece.

Those were wild and lively days. An acquaintance of Benito Mussolini brought them together with the great man, who wanted American capital to undertake a slum clearance project on the outskirts of Rome. The project eventually fell through, but perhaps it left Dole with one valuable conclusion, that even the most powerful and remote dignitaries are approachable under the right circumstances. He returned to New York in 1929 to become an insurance broker, in 1929 married a beautiful girl from Greenwich named Jane Ely, and settled down to a calmer life—including skiing.

A rebuff by the War Department was not at all to Dole's taste, but he was shrewd enough to know that military fat cats can be skinned in more than one way. In June 1940, he sent a circular letter to the ninety-three patrols of the National Ski Patrol System asking permission to offer their services directly to the War Department. The premise was rather vague. Either members of the patrol would train draftees in skiing, or the patrol itself might be organized into volunteer groups incorporated into the Army.

What Dole did not realize was that the first, faint stirrings of interest in skiing had already manifested themselves within the Army. During the winter of 1939 the commanding officer at Fort Snelling, Minnesota, in the cold and snowy country just outside Minneapolis–St. Paul, had obtained permission to start the most modest sort of ski training program. A young German immigrant named Hans Wagner was hired as instructor. There was no money for modern ski equipment—if indeed anyone beside Wagner knew that such equipment existed. The half-frozen GIs slid around the Fort Snelling parade ground on toestrap skis, using thin GI boots as substitutes for ski boots. The training program did get publicity, the Finnish war being under way, and perhaps that is what the Army was after.

At about the same time a young captain named Ridgely Gaither found himself transferred from field duty to the office in Washington of the Chief of Infantry, headed by Major General George A. Lynch. He was assigned to the Plans and Training Section (G–3). His job was to look into the matter of special troops that might be used in out-of-the way areas—exotic places such as mountains and jungles, on seashores where amphibious troops might land, and in the sky above the battlefields where parachutists or troop-laden gliders might float to earth to join in combat. Gaither's little cubbyhole office became the recipient of all sorts of ideas considered nutty by the higher command. After the Japanese attacked Pearl Harbor and overran the far Pacific, some correspondent (anonymous at this distance) wrote Mrs. Franklin D. Roosevelt suggesting a novel idea. Japanese, he said, gave off a different smell than American soldiers. Why not train war dogs to distinguish this smell, to swim ashore in advance of amphibious invaders and, by biting and barking, to reveal the whereabouts of the yellow devils? Whether Eleanor Roosevelt personally endorsed the idea, Gaither does not remember. But a special training center was set up on several small islands in Mobile Bay and staffed with Nisei (Japanese–American) soldiers from Hawaii. So many Nisei were bitten that a near-mutiny ensued. To top it all, it developed that the dogs would bite anyone, white or otherwise. The experiment was abandoned.

Gaither did achieve some support for the principle of jungle, amphibious and airborne warfare, but it took him longer to sell mountains as a possible battlefield. There was, Gaither recalls, "a mighty thin file" on the subject of mountains, snow and skiing —a handbook or two from European countries, and a few reports from military observers about the Finnish war. Nobody knew where to find Americans who were well-enough acquainted with skiing and climbing to fill in the gaps; though, in fact, there were plenty of them around. Nevertheless, Gaither was authorized to plan for three mountain divisions—the 10th, 12th and 14th—as well as for twelve others assigned to jungle, airborne and amphibious warfare.

Rescue from his mountain division dilemma, though he did

not know it, was on the way. Having received the approval of his ski patrol leaders, Dole wrote a short note to General Hugh Drum, commanding the First Army on Governor's Island—just a short ferry ride from his Wall Street office. On July 2, he received the following letter from Drum's aide-de-camp, Captain Christian Clarke, Jr.:

"The pressure of some other matters has delayed my study of your proposal regarding use of the Ski Patrol for which I am sorry.

"This morning I discussed the matter at length with the Chief of Staff, Second Corps Area, General Phillipson. He has had more experience than probably any other high-ranking Army officer in the subject of winter training of troops and is enthusiastic in his support of your proposal. However, in view of the orders for next winter's training, it would appear that the American Army will probably be concentrated in the South for training next winter. For this reason it would seem that the War Department does not contemplate any training of troops under winter conditions, such as one would find in the northeastern part of the United States. General Phillipson feels that you should communicate direct with the War Department regarding your proposal, and although he is heartily in accord with your idea, he feels that you will have a long uphill fight in your effort to sell the War Department on this plan.

"I regret that I have been unable to give you more help or encouragement as I personally heartily concur with your idea for the use of the National Ski Patrol. If there is anything further that I may do, please feel free to call on me and I shall be happy to assist you."

Dole answered four days later:

"As outlined to you, I am calling a meeting of an advisory group of members of the National Ski Patrol in the near future. At that time we will discuss fully and outline a program that we think and hope will be acceptable in Washington. I will not contact Washington until I have gone over with you whatever the outcome of our meeting may be.

"I anticipate, as you have pointed out to me, keen resistance to any such idea, but if the Army will not entertain it, I am seriously thinking of organizing a Voluntary Group myself and putting such Corps through a month's training next winter, with the aid of foreign teachers who are familiar with maneuvers as carried on in their own countries. If that has to be the case, it may be that I can wangle from the Army a few officers to instruct us in the use of the modern armaments that ski troops would be called upon to use. Again, I wish to repeat my appreciation for your cooperation and I definitely do not intend to lose track of you anyway. Please extend my kind regards to General Phillipson."

On July 7, the phone rang: Captain Clarke calling Dole to an appointment with General Phillipson. The next morning Dole and John Morgan took the ferry ride to Governor's Island. General Phillipson, a rotund man with a gruff manner, took them into his confidence.

"I suppose," he said, "I know more than anyone in the Army about the necessity for winter warfare training. I have been in command of Pine Camp [just outside Watertown, New York] in the winter. I know the effect of cold weather on troops. They simply hate to maneuver in subzero weather. When you need winter troops, you need them badly. This kind of force is not trained overnight either. I would gladly open the doors of the War Department for you, but it might do you more harm than good. They'd only say: 'There's Phillipson shooting off his face again.' "

"Okay, sir," said Dole. "Then we'll go to Washington and take our chances."

But before he made any further plans, Dole sat down at his typewriter and rattled off a letter to President Roosevelt offering the services of the National Ski Patrol in the recruitment of skiers for use as Army patrols in winter country.

As anyone familiar with the American military establishment is aware, all too often the left hand knoweth not what the right hand doeth. While Dole was beating on the doors of the War Department and Ridgely Gaither was frantically trying to find out how to set up the organizational structure of mountain divisions, the G–3 (Plans and Training Section) of the War Department was becoming more and more insistent about the need for winter troops.

"In view of the speed which has characterized European operations to date," said the G–3 memorandum dispatched to Marshall in August 1940, "no theater for the employment of American troops can be dismissed from consideration as fantastic. While it appears improbable at the moment, it is conceivable that our ability to fight in winter terrain might be of major, even decisive, importance. Obviously the desirable training objective is the immediate creation of divisions fully equipped and highly trained for this type of war. In view of the actualities of the situation, it is necessary that we begin this training on a small, more honestly on an inadequate, scale, but we can at least take the first steps to prepare for operations of this type." On August 6, the department ordered experiments to establish what changes from normal Army operations and equipment would be necessary to carry on winter warfare.

Morgan and Dole boarded the train to Washington, a few days later, without the slightest idea of how to gain entree to the War Department or to whom they might talk. The old "temporary" buildings on the Mall that housed the War and Navy departments were overrun with people with suggestions and recommendations. Few of them ever got beyond the reception desk.

At about Philadelphia, Dole roused himself from a brown study. "I've got it!" he said to Morgan. "I'll get hold of Stu Symington." Stuart Symington, later to serve as Secretary of the Air Force and as United States senator from Missouri, was a Yale classmate of Dole's, working for the government as a civilian member of a committee attempting to expedite the production of shells. Symington's name meant something at the War Department, for his father-in-law was Senator James W. Wadsworth of New York. Wadsworth was one of the sponsors of a bill establishing the draft. This was a prime project of President

Roosevelt's, and it brought Wadsworth into continuous contact with Harry H. Woodring, Secretary of War, and Louis A. Johnson, Undersecretary of War.

The hunch paid off. Symington introduced the two visitors from New York to his father-in-law. "You couldn't be more right about the ski troop idea," Senator Wadsworth said. "General Buckner in Alaska is screaming for winter-trained troops right now, and we haven't got them." He picked up the telephone and arranged an appointment for the next day with Clarence E. Huebner, a colonel on the General Staff.

Dole and Morgan sat up most of the night discussing how to present their case. "Seems to me," said Dole, "that we'd better have some information to offer about how ski troops are being used right now. You know, the Ski Club of Great Britain has formed a group of volunteers and they've been incorporated into the British Army. And the Scottish Ski Club has ski patrols to carry rations on skis to antiaircraft positions that are snowed in."

The next morning, just about the hottest of the summer, Dole and Morgan were ushered into Huebner's office. He was a dour man at best, and the blazing heat did nothing to improve his temper. Dripping sweat, he said, "Well, gentlemen, what did you wish to talk about?" Huebner listened only a few minutes before he pushed a button. "The Army's plans call for maneuvers in the South this coming fall and winter," he said, "so I'm afraid that cancels the possibility of winter training."

At which point, a Major Bruce walked in the door and ushered Dole and Morgan out. In Bruce's own office, he bombarded them with questions. Then he smiled and said, "Hell, we have a hundred guys a day like you. They even want us to try out guns that they say can shoot around corners." In turn, he pushed another button, and a young captain appeared to show Dole and Morgan out. Perhaps from politeness, the captain asked a few questions and then said, "If we were going to do anything about this, could you advise us on equipment?"

Yes, said Dole and Morgan, they could, and then Dole quickly said, "We'll be back in a month, sir." He didn't want another "We'll get in touch with you" answer.

What Dole and Morgan could not know was that the Army was frantically trying to bring its limited forces up to fighting fitness. Exotic ideas, such as ski and mountain troops, had their supporters in certain segments of the War Department, but they also had some bitter opponents. Among the latter was Brigadier General Lesley J. McNair, a senior staff officer in the office of the Chief of Infantry. His job was to train standard infantry divisions and to prepare them for standard types of combat in France or England or the Low Countries or wherever they might be needed. The idea of special troops, with the Army in such a desperately undermanned state, was nonsense to him. It remained so throughout the war, after he became head of the Army ground forces and thus one of the most powerful men serving Major General George C. Marshall, Chief of Staff of the Army. That was one reason why remote corps commanders such as General Phillipson could be enthusiastic while Washington staff men such as Colonel Huebner could be brusque.

His own enthusiasm chilled, Dole turned to Morgan to discuss how they could break through the barrier of indifference in Washington to someone—anyone—who might listen and concur. Their first thought was to collect all the information they could find on the subject of winter and mountain troops. Germany had them, France and Italy as well. For the next month they gathered all the information available. It made a fat dossier when they called on General Phillipson at Governor's Island. "I knew it would be difficult," he said. "Your only hope now is to see General Marshall. But you might make it. I think it is important you try."

But how to get to General Marshall? The resourceful Dole, as usual, came up with a connection. He knew Hayden Smith, a law partner of Henry L. Stimson, who had just succeeded Woodring as Secretary of War. Smith in turn put him in touch with an associate, Arthur Palmer, who had gone to Washington as a special assistant to Stimson. It was a fortunate ploy with some unexpected results—for though Dole did not know it, Stimson was an accomplished mountaineer. He had climbed in the Adirondacks, the Alps and the American Rockies around Glacier Park. He was also a member of the American Alpine Club, an association of distinguished mountaineers. Anything to do with high-altitude warfare was bound to interest him, and thus to interest his staff even more.

When Dole and Morgan returned to Washington, they met Palmer and Stimson's military aide in the secretary's outer office. What started as a polite conversation lasted two hours. Dole quoted General Phillipson's belief that if the Germans ever attacked they would follow the old British route up the St. Lawrence River, then through the Champlain and Hudson valleys to New York, severing the eastern seaboard from the rest of the country. The only place an enemy following this route could be stopped would be in the Adirondack and Green mountains, flanking Lake Champlain. Below, the country was so low and open that mechanized columns could move at will.

"Where the National Ski Patrol comes in," Dole said, "is as guerrillas. We have a lot of native mountain men in the Northeast. They know the woods, the back roads and the trails. They could be useful to regular Army troops as scouts or guides." The argument seemed to carry weight with Palmer and the military aide. As the conversation drew to an end, Dole decided to attack. "Mr. Palmer," he said, "we have to talk to General Marshall."

Palmer and the aide glanced at each other, and then the aide said, "Of course, I can't guarantee the outcome, but I think you have a sound premise and I shall report to the secretary on your behalf."

A few days later a messenger laid a telegram on Dole's office desk at 99 John Street, in downtown New York. It read:

TENTATIVE APPOINTMENT WITH GENERAL MARSHALL 10 O'CLOCK THURSDAY MORNING STOP LETTER FOLLOWING END. A. E. PALMER.

6

The Stars in Conjunction

ON THE WAY to Washington by train, the night of September 9, Dole and John Morgan consumed most of the trip debating what they might say that would impress General Marshall. They were, after all, only civilians, and Marshall was like the Dalai Lama to his staff—approachable only by those who had something significant to tell him. About the only civilians he saw regularly were his three superiors, the President of the United States, the Secretary of War, and the Undersecretary of War.

The best gambit Dole and Morgan could offer was the services of National Ski Patrols in the East as scouts, guides or guerrillas —natives who knew the woods, backroads and mountain trails, and thus could prevent an invader from outflanking American defense forces along the valley highways. They were still rehearsing their speeches as they walked up the steep flight of steps at the entrance to the State, War and Navy Buildings next door to the White House.

Marshall, cool in his summer dress uniform and blindingly polished cavalry boots, said only a few words of greeting, and then told an aide: "Ask Huebner to step in." (Marshall never called any officer in the armed services by his first name; some wits said he always addressed his wife as "Mrs. Marshall.")

Colonel Huebner, more tractable than when they last saw him, greeted Dole and Morgan cordially. For fifteen minutes all four talked about what American skiers could do to serve their country if given a chance. "As it happens," said Marshall, "we are leaving several divisions in the North this coming winter for winter training. You've raised some interesting questions, gentlemen. Thank you for coming. You will hear from me one way or another."

Things were falling rapidly into place. Less than a week later, Dole received a letter from E. S. Adams, the Adjutant-General.

"I am directed," it said, "to make further reference to a letter addressed by you to the President under date of July 18, 1940, relative to a plan to enlist skiers and train them, and outlining the nature of the organization of the National Ski Association.

"The Department appreciates the patriotic motive which prompted your letter to the President, and you are advised that its subject matter has been referred to the appropriate War Department agency for consideration. The Chief of Infantry, who is responsible for the training of infantry troops, is interested in your proposal, and you will doubtless hear from him direct."

Within another week, Dole did hear. On September 24, General Marshall wrote Dole:

"Your excellent paper on winter training has been referred to the G–3 Division of the General Staff for study.

"I am informed by the G–3 Division that two general plans are under study and in preparation; (1) the establishment of an agency for test and development of clothing and material for winter warfare operations, and (2) the procurement of skis and other equipment with which to begin ski instruction in certain divisions, initially for morale and recreational purposes. I must emphasize that both of these proposals are still in the study stage, that no decision has been reached, and that no information should be given to the press concerning these projects until officially released by the War Department.

"Should these general plans receive approval, it is probable that we should wish to call upon you for advice and assistance in the employment of expert civilian instructors and the procurement and development of equipment.

"It is also possible that the use of the ski patrol might be coordinated with general plans for the employment of patriotic civilians in Home Defense. This matter will be taken under study when the more immediate problems have been considered.

"I wish to thank you again for your personal interest in our National Defense and your generous offer of assistance in our cold weather projects."

About twelve days later, Colonel Nelson M. Walker, of the General Staff, met Dole and Morgan at the Yale Club in New York City, under instructions from General Marshall. "Johnnie" Walker appeared with Colonel Charles M. Hurdis, also of the General Staff. What they had to offer was a pilot force, a test force operating on skis. But there was a worm in the gift apple. The men in the pilot force would have to get by wearing GI-issue overshoes and skis with leather toestraps—no bindings. To skilled skiers like Dole and Morgan this raised the red flag. Politely but vehemently, they argued that soldiers would learn nothing, could only flounder about, and would become discouraged in a hurry. Walker listened tolerantly, and then said: "Remember that, in dealing with the Army, you must follow the old Polish saying: 'Nothing is ever eaten as hot as it is cooked.' Let's get our foot in the door, then we'll fight." So toestrap skis it was.

The next question was how to finance the advisory work the National Ski Patrol would carry on. The patrol was subsisting in a cubbyhole office with just one secretary. "How much do you think you'd need?" asked Walker. Morgan scribbled on a piece of paper and handed Dole a note reading, "$3,500." The latter gave it a quick glance, and said, "Sixty-five hundred dollars." Within a few days, the first installment of the money arrived, and the patrol moved into new, somewhat greater offices in the Graybar Building, in the Grand Central area.

In Washington, meanwhile, an agency had been set up in the office of the Quartermaster General to test and develop clothing and material for winter operations. The first expert summoned, a civilian, was Robert H. Bates, a distinguished alpinist, who had taken part in the ascent of Nanda Devi in the Himalayas with a British-American expedition and in the attempt of an American expedition to climb K2, second highest mountain in the world. He was soon joined by Albert H. Jackman, a captain in the Army reserve, with long skiing experience, and then by a very social civilian volunteer, John H. Tappin. Tappin was a fine skier, and for several years had been head of the ski clothing department at Brooks Brothers. He was the son of Mrs. Huntington Tappin, who arranged dinners and coming-out parties for important New York families.

Bates, a master of English at Exeter, was a quiet man with a streak of mischief. Experimental equipment poured into his office, including, one day, a new type of climbing rope. Doubling it, and hooking the doubled end to a solid piece of furniture in his office, he roped down from the second floor of one of the "temporary" World War I buildings on the Washington mall in which he was quartered. The secretary to General Jacques Doriot, the Assistant Quartermaster General, on the floor below, was looking idly out her window when she saw a man appear from overhead. She let out a bloodcurdling scream, and the general himself rushed in to look. By this time, Bates had reached the ground and was disentangling himself from the rope. "Do it again, Bates! Do it again!" cried the general. An order is an order, however couched, so Bates ascended to the roof and demonstrated his rappel to an admiring audience of secretaries and senior officers.

On November 9, another letter came from General Marshall:

"I have been informed by members of my staff of the cooperation rendered by the National Ski Association in the formulation of the War Department's plans for winter training.

"The tentative plans of the Winter Defense Committee of the National Ski Patrol appear to me to constitute a patriotic contribution to the National Defense. I understand these plans to be as follows:

"The personnel of the National Ski Patrol, acting as a volunteer civilian agency, to become fully familiar with local terrain; to locate existing shelter and to experiment with means of shelter, such as light tents, which may be found suitable for the sustained field operations of military ski patrol units; to perfect an organization prepared to furnish guides to the Army in event of training or of actual operations in the local areas; and to cooperate with and extend into inaccessible areas the antiaircraft and antiparachute warning services.

"The offer of the American Ski Association to furnish informal advice and assistance in the technique of skiing and the purchase of equipment is appreciated. Please extend to Mr. Langley and to the other officials of the Association working with you my personal thanks for your patriotic support."

A separate directive from the Secretary of War ordered the establishment of ski patrols within five divisions from coast to coast stationed in northern states. Selected men were to be taught the use of skis and snowshoes, and the fundamentals of campaign and traveling in the snow and high mountains. A Winter Warfare Board was established under the direction of Colonel Gaither.

Though the amateurs were gradually assuming a role of guidance in the Army's first efforts to create winter soldiers, the old system died hard. When Dole paid a visit to Washington to offer his services to the Winter Warfare Board, his prime worry was the kind of equipment that would be issued the troops. Gaither handed over a manual entitled, "Alaskan Equipment, Revised Edition, August 1914." Dole, a peppery and earnest man, flipped through the manual and said, "Junk it. It doesn't apply." And Gaither did, but not without asking for more current advice from the National Ski Association. That body formed a winter equipment committee in November, headed by Bestor Robinson, the most zealous experimenter with winter and mountain equipment anywhere in the United States. Other members included Langley and Dole (ex-officio), Alfred M. Lindley (who had climbed Mt. McKinley on skis), Douglas Burckett, of the Appalachian Mountain Club in Boston, Walter A. Wood, an expert on the Alaskan mountains, and Peter Hostmark, a Seattle ski-mountaineer.

The committee's job was a staggering one. Before World War II, there were an estimated 2,000,000 skiers in the United States (the figure seems optimistic and, in fact, was not based on concrete information). Most of them knew just enough to be able to ride a rope tow and to slide down a packed slope. The Army, by contrast, was interested only in skiers who could live out of their packs for many days on expeditions into rough country, in all kinds of weather. Such skiers probably numbered only a few hundred; any ski and mountain equipment manufacturer who tried to live off the business they generated would have starved. So skis, boots and clothing were manufactured from the civilian viewpoint, not the rough usage of the military. Lightweight cook-stoves, such as the Himalayan expeditions used, were not even manufactured in this country. Suitable rations, dehydrated and compactly packed, did not exist.

One of the committee's first jobs was to collect all the foreign manuals on winter warfare. Adams Carter, a master at Milton Academy, a fine Alpine climber and an able translator, made quick work of turning manuals from the European mountain armies into English. But these weren't of much help to begin with, for the emphasis was defense of the United States against invasion, not invasion by us of a foreign country. Thus in most parts of Europe soldiers in winter could rely on huts, barns and farmhouses for bivouacs, or at high altitudes could camp in crevasses or dig caves in the snow. The American West was roadless at high altitudes; soft, powdery snow would not com-pact itself for use as snow caves, and there weren't any glaciers complete with crevasses. Arctic and Antarctic expeditions yielded some clues, provided mainly by polar explorers such as Sir Hubert Wilkins and Vilhjalmur Steffansson. But Arctic expedi-tions were based on the use of sled dogs, with a slight assist from motorized equipment. There weren't enough sled dogs in the world to keep an Army supplied, let alone carry their own food, and on steep slopes in deep snow they bogged down. As for oversnow machines—none that were workable had been devel-oped by 1940. Similarly, mountain climbing and Himalayan ascents provided some hints but no workable solutions. The great climbs in the Himalayas were based on the use of porters, back-packing supplies from camp to camp and requiring weights well over the maximum military load.

The confusion took time to iron out. In late November 1940, the Army summoned a meeting to review the equipment problem at its headquarters on Commonwealth Pier, Boston. Colonel George Grice, representing the War Department, opened the meeting genially with the comment: "Gentlemen, I don't know a mukluk from a ski pole, but I know how to ask questions and to get the answers. I know we must have the proper equipment for this project to succeed." He soon found that even the skiers present—among them Dole, Robinson, Tappin, Livermore and Langley—couldn't agree on the properties of the various types of wood used in making skis. Grice, no dawdler, had the Army fly in a man from the Forest Laboratories in Madison, Wisconsin. Every aspect of skiing and ski equipment was discussed by specialists, and finally agreement was hammered out on basic items of equipment.

Such is the individualistic nature of skiers that the type of binding created a violent argument. Some of the volunteers wanted a leather strap binding, saying it was the easiest to put on and take off. Others wanted a steel cable binding—a little more difficult to take off, but one that held the skier's boot solidly on the ski when he was traveling downhill. The two Army representatives at this series of meetings were amused to discover that even the so-called experts could not agree.

The Equipment Committee, however, was lucky in its personnel. The chairman was Robinson, who had for years experimented with ski equipment, mountaineering equipment, and techniques for both sports. He was the first mountaineer to become involved with the ski troops, and in large part was responsible for the gradual shift of emphasis by the Army from cross-country skiing to mountain skiing, and then to a combination of skiing and climbing that would make the troops mobile whether or not there was snow on the ground.

Other members were added to the Equipment Committee: Charles M. Dudley of Hanover, New Hampshire, a specialist on ski equipment; Rolf Monsen, the Lake Placid ski instructor; and David Bradley of Madison, Wisconsin, who had served as an observer during the Finnish war.

Robinson and his colleagues, who traveled the whole of the High Sierra on skis, had developed equipment so light and compact that the total weight for camping on snow was reduced to fourteen pounds, plus two pounds of food per man per day. They even drilled holes in their toothbrush handles to cut down on weight, and they leaned toward exotic combinations of nuts and fruits—carefully assayed for protein and vitamin values—rather than the straightforward steak, ham and more conventional foods preferred by eastern ski-tourers.

When Robinson got deep into his job, he discovered that the lack of technical information was appalling—particularly to a Sierra Clubber who had devoted hours to the creation of specialized equipment. The capacity for warmth of a sleeping bag had never been measured; nobody knew how much eiderdown was required to secure comfort at a given low temperature. But so well and so effectively did the Equipment Committee work—backstopped in Washington by Bob Bates—that by late summer 1941, the Quartermaster General had approved specifications for rucksacks, sleeping bags, parkas, ski pants, gaiters, headbands, felt insoles, knives, boot toe protectors, mittens, ski tents, ski caps, white camouflage trousers, ski repair kit, snowshoes, climbers to be strapped on skis, poles, ski boots, stoves and even ski waxes.

This work had been helped along by actual experiments in the field. Paul Lafferty, Robinson, and a group of Sierra Club skiers made a two-week ski tour in the High Sierra near Bishop, California. Amid zero weather, blizzards and gale winds, they were able to try out projected items of equipment, to modify them in accordance with their experiences, and to make sound recommendations to the Quartermaster General. That same year Bates and Jackman made a spectacular trip to the Yukon to test equipment. The Air Force parachuted supplies into the mountains at eighty-mile intervals; Bates and Jackman, on skis or sometimes afoot, navigated a compass course through some of the wildest country on the continent and picked up every cache of supplies in sequence. It was a clear demonstration of what mountain-trained men could do.

The advent of Walter Wood led to a quickening of interest on the part of the American Alpine Club. Bates and John C. Case, president of the American Alpine Club, offered their services to the Army. Bates was commissioned, and later supervised the creation of much of the climbing and camping equipment used by the 10th Mountain Division. Case was a friend and former climbing companion of Secretary of War Stimson.

The mountain troop concept had begun to round itself out— but the linchpin of the whole slow, painful process of creating and equipping a division remained Minot Dole. He had already written thousands of letters connected with the formation of the ski troops, or mountain troops. He was to write thousands more before he was done. A man of extreme conscientiousness, obsessed by the necessity of providing the first mountain division in the United States Army, he worked a twenty-hour day at his typewriter and on the telephone.

7

Growing Pains

THE FINNS had been overrun by Russia before the winter of
1940–1941, and the British had also been driven out of Norway
by German mountain troops who overran their last foothold, the
northern port of Narvik. As the first snows frosted the topmost
tier of states, the commanders of six northern U.S. Army divisions sent out a call for the skiers tucked away in their ranks.
The Department of the Army had ordered winter training for
the 1st Division at Fort Devens, Massachusetts; the 44th Division
at Fort Dix, New Jersey; the 5th Division at Fort Custer, Michigan; the 6th Division at Fort Leonard Wood, Missouri; and the
3rd and 41st Divisions at Fort Lewis, Washington. The objective
was to set up a series of ski patrols that could, if necessary, serve
as the eyes for road-bound divisions—a compromise based upon
what the Finns had done in fighting the Russians. Selected men,
if possible woodsmen or skiers, were to be further trained in
skiing, snowshoeing and camping under extreme conditions in
the snow and high mountains (where these existed nearby).
Each patrol was given $1,200 to buy ski equipment locally—not
enough, of course, to equip each man completely, but enough so
that groups of men could be trained in turn.

The 26th Infantry Regiment, less one battalion, was desig-

nated by the 1st Infantry Division to undertake its training in
the Adirondacks, based on Plattsburgh Barracks, New York.
Every week, for nine successive weeks, ten officers and one hundred enlisted men rode Army trucks to Lake Placid for training
under Rolf Monsen, three times captain of the U.S. Olympic
jumping team. This was strictly cross-country training on the
rolling meadows and gentle woodland trails around Lake Placid.
The troops never got into the high Adirondack country where
downhill techniques would be required. There was some grumbling among civilians interested in the Army ski training program that the three officers and fifty-three men subsequently
formed into a patrol would be helpless if they ever had to fight
in mountainous Europe. But, in fact, the Army was thinking not
of war abroad; rather, of the defense of the continental United
States, particularly the eastern seaboard.

Some interesting judgments came out of the 1st Division training program: Not much training was needed to make soldiers
proficient on snowshoes. Teaching troops to ski was also com-
paratively easy. (It was, because these troops didn't get into the
mountains.) Ski patrols should operate as horse cavalry had in
the past. (And, in fact, this was exactly how patrols of the 10th
Mountain Division operated in combat.) The soldiers liked the
ski and snowshoe training. It was a pleasant change from close-
order drill, and it took them away from daily camp discipline.
Their commander, Colonel John Muir, liked it too.

"I believe that ski training is an asset," he wrote in a subsequent report. "Like the Texan's six-shooter, you may not need
it, but if you ever do, you will need it in a hurry, awful bad."

The 6th Division sent out two companies to Fort Warren,
Wyoming, and one to Fort Snelling, Minnesota. A lucky patrol of
eleven officers and eleven enlisted men received the benefit of
training by one of America's finest downhill ski racers, Alfred
H. Lindley of Minneapolis, assisted by Glen Stanley, another
capable racer. More useful knowledge came from this training:
Each battalion should have one ski patrol. All rifle companies
should be ski-trained and equipped. And, a significant note,
"troops must be stationed at places known to be suitable for

snowshoeing and skiing." This accurately forecast the course of the mountain troops, even though nobody but a few high officers in Washington knew that such an organization was even being considered.

The 5th Division trained at Camp McCoy, Wisconsin, there being insufficient snow at Fort Custer—and here, again, a significant step toward the mountain troop concept was taken. Captain Jackman, a reserve officer and an excellent skier, organized a Winter Training Board to make sure that no aspect of training was neglected. From this later grew a Mountain and Winter Warfare Training Board that was to guide the mountain infantry in its formative days.

The 44th Division had the most rip-roaring time on skis. A twenty-man ski patrol was formed under the direction of Lieutenant Eric C. Wikner, formerly a competitive skier in Sweden, with long experience in winter camping. To his delight, just a few days before the patrol was due to set off for the snow country, Harald G. Sorensen was called up for duty with the division as a private. Sorensen had been a ski jumper in Norway and coach of the U.S. Olympic ski-jumping team. This assured him a post as coach to the patrol, and initiated a significant precedent: Enlisted men as well as officers could be used to train skiers. When the 87th Mountain Infantry got into full swing, the enlisted men did most of the teaching and training, for only a scant handful of officers had ever had prior experience on skis. Sorensen, a gusty extrovert with a thick Scandinavian accent and a voice that could be heard for miles across the snowdrifts, was an inspiration to the men he trained. They never forgot him.

The 44th Division patrol went to Old Forge, in the southwestern Adirondacks, an area notable for deep snow, mildly similar to the rolling hills of Finland. For three and a half weeks the men camped out in subzero temperatures, as low as 20 below zero Fahrenheit. Sleeping bags and tents were tested, and an immense amount of valuable information was compiled. Skis were a rarity in this section of the Adirondacks, where the snowshoe was prized as the only means of winter transport into remote areas. So, naturally, there was a good deal of argument at night in the local bars between the snowshoeing lumberjacks and the skiing soldiers. This culminated in a challenge: "Let's see which are faster—skis or snowshoes."

The snowshoers laid out the five-mile course, which included a lot of steep climbs and thick, brushy terrain. They didn't realize that ski wax could conquer the steep places, and that skis could shoot down hills that snowshoers had to plod down. Hans Wagner, the Fort Snelling teacher, won in forty-eight minutes; Wikner was second in 49 minutes, even though he broke a ski near the end of the course and had to pole himself in on one ski. In a second race, the natives enlisted a fleet Abenaki Indian snowshoer, Maurice Denis, but Wagner still won by six minutes.

Mock wars kept the normally snowbound Old Forgers agog. A sham battle was staged on Little Moose Mountain; patrols covered thirty miles daily, and finally the forces of right (the U.S.) triumphed over the unnamed enemy. The climactic battle was staged at Maple Ridge, on the edge of the village, and was witnessed by 3,000 impressed Adirondack natives—just about all the population within a radius of thirty miles. The troops had traveled twenty-five miles that day, carrying forty-five pound packs, and arriving fit to fight.

When the Fort Dix patrol marched to the train on March 7, 1941, the whole town turned out, a drum and bugle corps whanged out patriotic tunes, and the citizenry was close to tears: So much excitement hadn't come to Old Forge in years. Somewhere down the line toward New York, the conductor handed a telegram to Wikner: "GOODBYE, LIEUTENANT, AND GOOD LUCK. REGARDS TO ALL YOUR BOYS. THE VILLAGE MISSES YOU ALREADY AND WANTS YOU BACK SOON." It was signed by J. F. Grady, president of the Old Forge Winter Sports Association. A little later in the spring, the patrol displayed itself to a somewhat larger and more sophisticated audience, marching in ski clothes and boots, with skis at right shoulder arms, down Fifth Avenue, in the Army Day parade, before Governor Herbert H. Lehman, Lieutenant General Hugh F. Drum, and Mayor Fiorello LaGuardia.

The two most spectacular patrols were those conducted in the

Pacific Northwest by the 3rd and 41st Divisions. Eighteen men from the 15th Infantry Regiment, 3rd Division, moved up to Longmire, under the slopes of Mt. Rainier. Quartered in a garage, they spent a month and a half on the flanks of Rainier, traveling through snow ten feet or deeper. Captain Paul R. Lafferty, former University of Oregon ski coach, was technical adviser; Lieutenant John B. Woodward, a University of Washington racer, was chief instructor. Though practically none of the trainees had previous experience on skis, they achieved a garrison finish through terrain of unusual beauty—a circumnavigation of Mt. Rainier, crossing half a dozen of its glaciers, passing through avalanche country, on a trip that took them two weeks. This long, tiring but spectacular ski tour has rarely been repeated since the war.

The 41st Division patrol had equally rugged training, using a CCC camp three miles outside Mt. Rainier National Park at Ashcroft. Sergeant Karl Hinderman, a professional instructor and former racer, really gave his protégés a workout. By the end of February 1941, when individual ski training had been completed, the patrol was ordered to cross the wild Olympic Mountains from west to east—up the Quinalt River and down the Dosewalips River, a distance of forty miles. This was shorter than the Mt. Rainier trip but more of a challenge—up narrow canyons, across windblown peaks, and down through the rain forests. And again the patrol paid dividends in creating doctrine for training and equipping soldiers. The War Department had no idea at all about the complexities of ski equipment. Some of the men had been issued skis without steel edges. These splintered and the edges became so rounded that soldiers could scarcely make a turn without sliding off the trail. Others who had steel-edged skis came through effectively and with less physical wear and tear.

The next test for the patrol, which taught equally valuable lessons, was a two-week trip along the northern end of the Olympics, rarely visited in winter. Men and equipment faltered under the strain of a project too severe for all but the most rugged or experienced. Civilian-made boots and bindings, designed for packed-slope skiing, fell apart; soldiers collapsed from exhaustion or limped on blistered feet, and eight of them were sent back to Fort Lewis. The other eighteen officers and men came out on their own skis—weary, faces blackened by the sun, but satisfied with having completed a mission more demanding than any that might be required in battle.

By the end of the winter, the Army had ample evidence that soldiers *could* be trained to ski, and that a mountain division *could* be created in a nation where skiing was still a *rara avis*. Men with no prior experience, if physically fit and athletically skilled, could be made into competent skiers, even instructors, in two months. By reverse token, even the most proficient downhill skier, accustomed to packed slopes, had to be trained in winter camping and toughened physically in order to carry a pack whose weight averaged fifty-five pounds across countryside where no tows or lifts existed to ease the uphill struggle.

The first of many lovely trips now brightened the life of those associated with the Army's winter program. In April 1941, Captain Lafferty was detailed to accompany Bestor Robinson and a party of experienced civilian skiers on a touring expedition in the High Sierra near Bishop, California. In zero weather, blizzards and gale winds—not to overlook a lot of warm spring sunshine and beautiful powder snow—the expedition tested tents, sleeping bags and other items proposed for Army use, and came up with suggestions that were passed along to the Quartermaster General. Also in April, the Army inched one step closer to the creation of a mountain division. Colonels Hurdis and Walker, along with Robert S. Monahan of the U.S. Forest Service, were ordered to study high-altitude sites in the west suitable for a one-division camp housing 15,000 men, where year-round training in winter and mountain maneuvers would be available.

The best choice seemed to be West Yellowstone, Montana, on the edge of Yellowstone National Park. It fulfilled all the requirements—access over a good railroad line, plenty of flat ground for barracks and artillery practice, and a pleasant community close at hand. But this ideal selection was frustrated by a rare fowl, the nearly extinct trumpeter swan. Trumpeters nested within the park; artillery and so many humans tramping about would disturb them. Frederic Delano, uncle of President Franklin Delano Roosevelt, a power in the Wildlife Conservation Committee, led the fight against the Army, and West Yellowstone was given up as a possible site. Whether the President himself indicated any concern about the trumpeter swan, or whether the consanguinity of Frederic Delano was responsible, nobody knows.

Colorado appeared to be the next best choice. West Yellowstone was about a mile above sea level; in Colorado it was possible to find sites 9,000 feet high. The requirements were revised to call for an area sufficient to house 20,000 men, accessible by railroad and highway, with adequate fuel supplies nearby and water on the spot, containing sufficient area for maneuvers and artillery ranges. The choice narrowed down to three sites—Aspen, on a rather decrepit branch railroad line; Wheeler, eighteen miles from the nearest railroad at Leadville; and Pando, a whistle stop just north of Tennessee Pass, at 9,200 feet elevation on the main line of the Denver and Rio Grande Railroad and on a main highway, U.S. 24. Aspen, fortunately for its future, was ruled out because of insufficient space; Wheeler because of remoteness.

Pando, which consisted of a station overlooking the beaver meadows of the Eagle River, thus started on its way to transitory fame. Most of the land was within the Arapaho National Forest, and would cost the Army nothing; the annual snowfall was supposed to be one of the heaviest in Colorado. The principal disadvantage—and some disadvantage it turned out to be—was the lack of social life for the troops. Leadville, eighteen miles away, was a somnolent mining town, but in its time it had been a riproaring honky-tonk, where prostitution was regarded as one of the civilized amenities. It seemed all too likely that the ladies would be moving in as soon as the troops did. Beyond that, the population was less than 1,500, and soldiers off-duty would have swamped it. Denver was 150 miles away by rail, entailing a six-hour trip through the Grand Gorge, and thus cutting down sharply on liberty time. The inspection board nevertheless recommended Pando.

Within the War Department, a private battle was going on between those who insisted on the need for a mountain division and those who felt it could wait. Funds for a mountain division camp were withheld "until later." General Harry Twaddle, frustrated in his efforts, wrote a sharply worded letter pointing out that, while tests of *winter* warfare clothing and equipment had been carried out, "nothing has been done along the line of *mountain* warfare." Lieutenant Colonel John M. Lentz backed him up: "All concerned agree in need for organization of the Mountain Division." Lieutenant Colonel Mark W. Clark, G–3, added more important support, writing General McNair: "Recommend we concur; at least we may get one more division; its proposed equipment, including particularly artillery, is such that it could readily be moved by air."

On August 5, General McNair answered with an emphatic "No!" While mountain divisions existed abroad, he doubted the need for them in the United States Army. The acerb McNair put his finger on one flaw in the mountain division concept—the inefficiency of its transport, with 7,983 pack mules and only 369 motor vehicles. Each howitzer of the division artillery involved 68 artillerymen and 68 animals. His alternate suggestion was the development of an infantry battalion and an artillery battalion, "capable of operating effectively in mountainous terrain."

That same day, Lieutenant Colonel Leonard S. Gerow of the General Staff Corps sent along to higher echelons a report from the American military attaché in Italy. The Italians had invaded the Balkans the summer before, and by midwinter had fled in confusion before a Greek counterattack, which drove them into the mountains of Albania. "The Italian high command," said the report, "could only throw piecemeal into the operations infantry divisions of the line as fast as they could be gotten to Albania. These divisions were not organized, clothed, equipped, conditioned, or trained for either winter or mountain fighting. The result was disaster. Twenty-five thousand were killed; ten thousand were frozen; large numbers made prisoners; loss in morale and prestige were irreparable."

The report concluded: "One of the most important lessons learned from this is that an army which may have to fight anywhere in the world must have an important part of its major units especially organized, trained, and equipped for fighting in the mountains and in winter. Such units cannot be improvised hurriedly from line divisions. They require long periods of hardening and experience, for which there is no substitute for time."

It was this memorandum that apparently tipped the scales. On October 22, 1941, Dole received letters from Secretary of War Stimson and from General Marshall announcing that on November 15, 1941, the 1st Battalion (Reinforced) 87th Infantry Mountain Regiment would be activated at Fort Lewis, Washington. That date in November was just twenty-two days before America found itself at war.

8

"Minnie's Ski Troops"

NOW AMERICA HAD ITS FIRST SKI TROOPS. *The New Yorker*, in its "Talk of the Town" section on February 21, 1942, quite accurately referred to them as "Minnie's Ski Troops," but at the very beginning nobody knew whose they were or what they were supposed to do. Three Regular Army officers had been assigned to the 87th. The commander was a taciturn, red-haired lieutenant colonel of cavalry, Onslow S. Rolfe, as much a stranger to skis as to mountains. The War Department had chosen him, he discovered later, because he came from New Hampshire, "a snow state." What they didn't know, he subsequently revealed, was that he had left New Hampshire at the age of six. Robert L. Cook and Robert Tillotson, both majors, had been transferred from Chilkoot Barracks near Seward, Alaska. The Army for several years previous had conducted winter warfare exercises there, with the troops shod in overshoes and waddling about on snowshoes. A fourth officer, on temporary duty, was Captain Jackman. He had been detached temporarily from the Quartermaster General's office to preside over field tests of new ski and mountain equipment, The NCOs, all transferred from other divisions, were presided over by a short-tempered long-timer, Sergeant-Major Fred Jones.

93

The day after the Japanese attacked Pearl Harbor, just twenty-two days after the 87th was activated, the first recruit reported. Appropriately, he was a ski racer from Dartmouth named Charles B. McLane who arrived with his own rucksack, own skis, clad in civilian clothes and wearing his green Dartmouth ski team sweater with a huge white "D" plastered on it. "I'm supposed to report to the mountain troops," he said. "Son," said the sergeant who welcomed him, "you *are* the mountain troops." That wasn't completely accurate. A private whose name nobody remembers, perhaps because he wasn't a skier, had already been assigned to tend furnaces in the regimental area.

A cadre of officers and men from the 3rd Division, the California National Guard, the 41st and 44th Infantry, along with assorted GIs who had heard of the formation of the 87th, soon flowed in. With them came three excellent company commanders, all reserve officers—Captain Lafferty (A Company), Captain Henry Hampton (B Company) and Captain Ross Wilson (C Company). Lafferty had years of racing and cross-country experience behind him; Hampton and Wilson were both outdoorsmen, brought up in the western mountains. As transfers filled the three companies, the ski troops soon lost their western orientation and became heavily Yankee.

Still, despite the best efforts of the National Ski Patrol, the Army was far short of the 4,000 men it wanted. At this point, in the early winter of 1941, Dole was asked to Washington and asked for men to flesh out the 87th. "We need them," they said. "Can you get them?"

"You cut the red tape," Dole replied, "and we'll get them. How many do you need, and how soon?"

The answer was, "Twenty-five hundred in sixty days."

A written contract between the National Ski Association and the Army made the Ski Patrol an official recruiting agency—the only civilian group thus designated. Every prospective draftee who wanted to join the 87th had to fill out a questionnaire and to submit three letters of recommendation from responsible individuals.

When I applied, in March 1942, the three letters came from

my employer, Joseph Medill Patterson, publisher of the New York *Daily News;* the managing editor of the *Daily News,* and the Episcopal bishop of Minnesota. Kay Boyle, the author, swept in with her husband, Baron George von Franckenstein, nephew of the former Austrian ambassador to the Court of St. James's. Peter Pringsheim, nephew of Thomas Mann, was sponsored by some eminent names in literature and teaching. Walter Prager, former Dartmouth ski coach, presented, among others, a letter from the president of the college. Private Leonard Woods whose mother was the first commander of the WACs, appeared in a GI dress jacket tailored to measure by J. Press. One irate father, whose son's application was delayed in processing, wrote Dole to say that if prompt action did not occur, "I shall be forced to write my friend, General Marshall."

There were less prominent applicants too, for the criterion was a broad one. The guideline was ability in skiing or mountaineering, but outdoorsmen, cowboys, woodsmen—anyone capable of spending a night in the winter woods without dying of exposure or fright—was welcome. The U.S. Forest Service and the National Park Service contributed more than a score of rangers. Some of them, after the war, became park superintendents or executives of the two services. The skiers included Torger Tokle, the national ski jumping champion, who, it developed, knew nothing whatever about downhill skiing and had to be taught the techniques. Dole's office was inundated with letters, some touching, some funny, some deadly serious.

Aubrey Spann, a Colorado ranger, wrote the supporting letter for Private Jack B. Bain, at the time in basic training:

"Our ranches in the Gunnison Valley are from eight to nine thousand feet above sea level. It is not unusual to have three to four feet of snow with temperature from 35 to 45 degrees below.

"Jack B. Bain grew up on a neighboring ranch, and many times I've been in cow camp with him in late fall when the going was pretty tough, but never do I remember of hearing a complaint from him.

"He has been handling horses all his life, as that is a major part of our business here.

"Jack has always been a good square shooter, always willing to do more than his share if need be. I know he is honest and sincere and no matter where you place him he will be a top hand."

Private Elmer Wallace Johnson, of Houston, was sponsored by his brother Floyd, who wrote:

"Pvt. Elmer Wallace Johnson was raised on a farm far from modern conveniences. He has been taught to live from the many things Nature put on this Earth. He can find food and shelter when the snows have fallen and everything is frozen over. He can tell the direction he is going when there is no sun or moon to go by. He knows how to catch and kill small game without the use of a gun, and to sleep warm without blankets or cover of any kind.

"All these things he can do, I taught him myself. His Brother, Floyd G. Johnson."

Horace G. Stafford, in basic training at Camp Roberts, California, wrote: "Last year I was in college . . . and decided to join the ski troops . . . and you sent me a blank to fill out. Boy, I was really rarin' to go—but! a certain lil' gal I knew in college winked her eye and wriggled a little and before I knew it I was standing at an altar saying, 'I do.' When I thought I had better send my application in, the little woman said (quote), You are *not* going to join the ski troops and get your neck busted! (unquote). Furthermore, she tore the application up and gave me definite orders to have the generals put me in the air corps when I got drafted, so here I am in the infantry. . . . Seriously, I am very happily married and I love my wife very much, but she doesn't seem to understand how I feel about skiing.

"Shoot the application out here and if I get in the mountains I'll think of some way of telling my wife. I think she'll understand, however, because she knows how much I love the snow and rocks."

Private R. J. Estee, in the artillery at Fort Bragg, North Carolina, wrote: "I *know* I could be an excellent skier. All I ask is just one short chance."

Private William A. Taylor, Jr., at Camp Custer, Michigan,

ABOVE: *Camouflaged troops of the 87th Infantry Mountain Regiment in training above Paradise Inn, Mt. Rainier National Park.*

BELOW: *A rest break on the slopes of Mt. Rainier, complete with K rations and lemonade from a canteen. The cumbersome ski boots were soon phased out in favor of a ski/mountain boot with cleated sole, suitable for both climbing and skiing.* [PHOTO BY U.S. ARMY SIGNAL CORPS]

RIGHT: *There were no mountains at Fort Lewis, so Sgt. Walter Prager, the noted Swiss ski racer and climber, set up some notched logs simulating a mountain wall, known as the "Pragerwand."*

BELOW: *Sgt. Peter Gabriel, a former Swiss guide and ski teacher, belays a trainee who is slowly working his way up a mountainside in the Tatoosh Range, across the valley from Mt. Rainier.*

ABOVE: *"Through these portals pass the most beautiful mules in the world."*

LEFT: *The founder of the Ski Troops, "Minnie" Dole, 1942.*

ABOVE: *A ski patrol in Italy—T/4 Robert L. Hackman phones back information about the progress of a patrol deep into the thinly held mountain lines of the enemy.* [U.S. ARMY PHOTOGRAPH]

BELOW: *The Weasel, the first successful over-the-snow vehicle, tows a patrol of the 86th Mountain Infantry to its starting point.* [U.S. ARMY PHOTOGRAPH]

ABOVE: *Medical corpsmen of the 10th Mountain Division bring a wounded soldier down from the top of a ridge in the Apennines campaign, 1945.* [U.S. ARMY PHOTOGRAPH]

BELOW: *Crossing a stream on skis—not an easy feat! Pfc. William C. Douglas leads a patrol of the 10th MD in Italy, 1945. By then, troops were already equipped with laminated skis, the forerunner of today's plastic and metal "sandwich" skis.* [U.S. ARMY PHOTOGRAPH]

ABOVE: *Lake Garda, from the road just south of the town of Garda, where the column struck the first roadblock. A U.S. M-10 tank destroyer (76mm AT gun) is at right.* [SKETCH BY GEORGE EARLE]

BELOW: *Verona falls to troops of the 85th Mountain Infantry; the Alps lie ahead.* [U.S. ARMY PHOTOGRAPH]

ABOVE: *The small cluster of farm buildings called Toca, where the 87th Mountain Regiment awaited H-hour. In the foreground, Italian "Alpini," with their feathered hats, seconded to the U.S. Army to lead the mules.* [SKETCH BY GEORGE EARLE]

BELOW: *On Riva Ridge, the 126th Mountain Engineers erected an aerial tramway, reducing the trip up or down from four hours to four minutes. Hundreds of lifts based on this principle now dot the slopes of the United States.* [U.S. ARMY PHOTOGRAPH]

ABOVE: *GI in the mountains, building a snow cave.* [PHOTO BY U.S. ARMY MOUNTAIN & WINTER WARFARE BOARD]

BELOW: *A Weasel in action in the high mountains.* [JOHN JAY PHOTO]

complained: "Here in this camp the land is level all around and there is no way of keeping the cold winds from travelling through here. I was born and reared in the mountains, and I'd sooner be in the mountains than on level, sandy ground."

Along with these letters from the hopeful came others from foresters, hunters and trappers. Private First Class John Kowalski, at Camp Carson, Colorado, felt qualified—and was—because he grew up in northern Montana, hunting deer and bear and trapping in the mountains on skis and snowshoes and guiding hunting parties.

Private Lincoln C. White, at Camp Wolters, Texas, had hiked and climbed in the Wasatch Mountains of Utah and the Teton and Wind River Ranges in Wyoming. Private Joseph Meyers, at Fort Benning, spent six winter months in a CCC camp in the mountains, and Clyde E. Quick, awaiting induction, noted that "I have ridden horses, punched cattle, and supervised work on the family 4,000-acre cattle ranch at Chowchilla, in the foothills of the Sierra Nevada."

The letters came flooding in. LeRoy P. Lawhead reported he had spent "considerable time in Alaska, mainly off of the coast of the Bering Sea, the Bristol Bay region, and in the Aleutian Ils., mainly Unalaska. . . . Some skiing with what we call the bush ski in which one or two sled dogs pull and are in harness and held with a leash."

Richard Calvelage couldn't ski, but had done much trapping. "The principal animal trapped in that area was the muskrat, although a considerable number of coon, opossum and skunk are present."

Private Barry R. Bauman, at Camp Hood, Texas, had been a logger and a lumberman since he was old enough to work. "In the past five years, I have built two sawmills and one planing mill." A supporting letter noted that "he is a natural leader of working men, and can do anything in a saw mill or logging camp from donkey punching to high climbing."

And then there was a letter from Portsmouth, New Hampshire, endorsing Private Stanley Chase Pingree: "He is an excellent skier and has the stamina to be one. He has always been a natural athlete and has never had to strive to be good at any sport. He just plain IS. I am not trying to get rid of my husband, but I do feel that my temporary loss will be your great gain." (Signed) Elinor Manscom Pingree.

The flood continued—boy scouts, boys from the country, and just plain dissatisfied soldiers with no particular qualification. Private Hollis Parson was endorsed by a letter from Lon B. Clawer, Pecan Gap, Texas, as "sturdy, quiet, sensible . . . I believe you will find him able and willing to do anything he promises to do. *Try him.*"

Leo Nowak, of Iron Mountain, Wisconsin, "used to go to school on skis nearly every day. He wore out two pairs. In winter when the roads were blocked with big drifts Leo used to get the mail from town 7 miles away and on Sunday used to go to church on skis and sure made good time."

Richard Messenger's endorsement was a little less related to skiing. E. R. Johnson recommended him for skill in games such as Capture the Flag and Steal the Bacon.

Private John E. Nelson went higher up for a recommendation, to C. M. Milton, superintendent of the Great Northern Paper Company at Greenville, Maine, who said he "has worked in the woods as a Swamper."

Sandy L. Bain's recommend came from Lewis F. Binning, of Folsom, California: "All of Mr. Bain's life was spent on a stock ranch at 8,000 feet elevation where the only means of travel to the post office and outside world for about four months or more each winter was on skis. . . . His spare time in the winter was spent on skis, running a trap line, hunting down the sheep-killing coyotes and other predatory animals."

Harold J. Loudon enclosed the following endorsement: "My Dear Son: You ask for a recommend. I think you are fit for the mountain troops. You always were a good boy and a hard worker. And I also think you are a brave boy and willing to do the work that is set before you. Your Mother."

One applicant had a sponsor whose sense of humor ran away from him. "It has been my misfortune," the sponsor wrote, "to know Mr. —— for a considerable number of years, and while it is true that he played hockey during his high school years and did get some minor reputation for his ability, the truth of the matter . . . is that he was so dumb and so much older than his classmates that he was practically a full-grown man playing against children. He does ski a little, drinks a lot, is a lousy dancer but a good painter and paperhanger. So is Hitler. I should be most willing to provide additional information of a similar nature should you so desire. (Signed) Carlton Chambers."

Dole fired back a sharp reply: "I judge that your sense of humor got the better of you when you sent in your letters of recommendation. I therefore return them to you and would appreciate greatly your sending in the one that applies, as we are terribly shorthanded in this office, and furthermore, if I send any punks such as you describe to the mountain troops it will only react to the disfavor of the National Ski Patrol System." The chastened Chambers sent a more conventional letter, and the man was accepted.

All through the early winter, as the coastal rains drummed down, transferred soldiers continued to flow into Fort Lewis. Among them was Private First Class Dyson Duncan, son of the president of Lea and Perrins. Duncan soon decided that he wanted his wife, the former Millie Stokes, to join him with their children. Money being no object, he leased the most commodious house in nearby Steilacoom. Unknown to him, the commanding general of Fort Lewis was considering the same house. When he finally decided to pay the price, he was astounded when the rental agent said: "Sorry, general, but Private First Class Duncan has already leased the house." That was the general's first inkling that men with money and social position preferred to join the ski troops as privates rather than to accept a direct commission as an officer in some other branch of the service.

The first professional ski teacher and certified Swiss mountain guide arrived shortly after Duncan in the person of Sergeant Peter Gabriel, former head of the ski school at Cannon Mountain, New Hampshire. Next came Sergeant Arnold Fawcus, head of the ski school at Yosemite National Park. They arrived looking for snow; all they found was rain and fog. Then began the

song and story period of the mountain troops, for Colonel Rolfe
received permission to lease Paradise Lodge and Tatoosh Lodge,
two government hotels at 5,000 feet elevation in Mt. Rainier
National Park, just sixty-two miles from the fort. Skiing started
from the second-floor windows. The snow depth ran twenty to
thirty feet.

"Ah, Paradise!" Men slept, in some cases, in individual bedrooms as companies rotated from Fort Lewis to the mountain
and back again. Soldiers in white camouflage uniforms fought
mock wars under the towering dome of Rainier. They couldn't
even use blank ammunition for fear of disturbing the wildlife.
It was a period of wonderful camaraderie. No matter how much
Colonel Rolfe kept insisting that the men were military skiers,
and thus different from recreational skiers, the spirit was more
like a college reunion than a military encampment: as witness
the 87th Mountain Infantry Glee Club, whose members included
McLane, Richard F. W. Whittemore, Second Lieutenant John
C. Jay, a lineal descendant of the first Chief Justice, and Ralph
Bromaghin, a Sun Valley ski instructor.

Army equipment for mountain troops was still only partially
developed, and, on maneuvers, rations, a tent, sleeping bag, extra
boots, extra clothing and a rifle with bayonet ran to roughly
ninety pounds, a staggering load. The glee club satirized this
backbreaking weight in a song, "Ninety Pounds of Rucksack," to
the tune of "Bell Bottom Trousers." The last verse summed up
the college spirit:

> For if you have a daughter, bounce her on your knee;
> But if you have a son, send the bastard out to ski!
> CHORUS:
> Singing ninety pounds of rucksack, a pound of grub or two;
> And he'll schuss the mountain like his daddy used to do.

It was Paradise that sold the mountain troops: pictures of
tanned soldiers in white camouflage suits, with the great white
ice cream cone of Rainier rising behind them, with miles of open
downhill running. For those who joined up after the winter of
1941–1942 it wasn't that glamorous, but through all the years of

training there were special expeditions designed to make any mountaineer happy. Nowhere else in the Army, certainly, could a soldier draw pay to make a summer climb of Rainier, up through the crevasses and past the snow cornices to the 14,408-foot summit, where smoking fumaroles served as a reminder that Rainier was not a dead volcano but a dormant one. To test equipment Jackman and others from the 87th climbed Mt. McKinley, highest on the continent, and then Mt. St. Elias, second highest in Canada.

In July 1942, under Major Robert Tillotson, five officers and forty men were suddenly delivered to the Columbia Icefields in the Canadian Rockies. Once there, they completed in twenty-six days a road to the foot of the Saskatchewan Glacier. Once set up in barracks they were told their mission, to build the first roadway in the world up a glacier to the level floor of the icefields. There, surrounded by some of the highest peaks in Canada, they were to help Studebaker test a new oversnow vehicle known as the Weasel. The whole project was secret; the location had been chosen so no German spy could find out what was going on. Under the supervision of Private Duncan, crevasses were bridged with logs, and replaced as the movement of the glacier required. Soon, trucks were roaring up to an altitude of 8,000 feet, where a cluster of metal Nissen huts constituted the highest Army encampment in the world.

Naturally, nobody told the members of the detachment how it all came about; nobody told them they had Winston Churchill to thank for five months of good chow from Studebaker, five months of skiing on the *névé* and the glaciers that dropped down like curtains from peaks such as Castleguard, Athabaska, Snow Dome, Kitchener and Columbia; five months of snow and ice climbing, starting from a height denied peacetime mountaineers. Churchill was a man who worshipped oddball projects such as the Commando invasion of Dieppe, which led to a disaster, and the undermanned invasion at Anzio, which nearly did. The stars in their courses brought him together with a half-mad scientist named Geoffrey Pyke, who proposed the development of oversnow vehicles to be dropped into Norway in November 1942.

There they would attack the power plants where heavy water was being made, the assumption being that heavy water was part of the German atomic energy program.

Pyke sold the idea to Churchill through Earl Mountbatten. The vehicles were to be small and light enough to be carried by a Lancaster bomber, tough enough to live through an air drop, and fast enough so German ski troops could not capture them. The whole thing was a crash program that did not start until April 1942, in the process being priority over development of the B–17 bomber for ninety days. Pyke had proposed that the machines be run by a pair of Archimedean screws, pulling the machine ahead as they revolved. Designers for the Office of Scientific Research and Development settled instead on a caterpillar type with wide rubber tracks. Though the Weasel had a habit of throwing the tracks on a fast turn, it did eventuate as a tough, speedy little vehicle. The only trouble was that nobody had told Air Marshal Harris, whose planes were to do the air drops. When he heard about it, he said, "No." The whole project was based on Churchill's enthusiasm, not on scientific tests. The Weasel did do a good job in the Italian Apennines, but scarcely one worth the millions of dollars invested in it.

Pyke, not chastened, then went through Churchill to talk the Canadian Army into Project Habakkuk. This involved the creation of an ice island, complete with propulsion, to serve as a floating carrier for planes in the Atlantic. The ice was to be reinforced with straw so that submarine torpedoes might knock off chips but could not sink the island—particularly since it included a refrigerating plant to keep the ice from melting as the Atlantic warmed. The Canadians did build one of these monstrosities in Lake Patricia, near Jasper, Alberta, before discovering that it would be cheaper to build a standard aircraft carrier out of steel. Pyke was abruptly retired by Mountbatten from his advisory role, and thereafter committed suicide.

Sworn to secrecy about the Weasel, members of the detachment came under the command of an able young first lieutenant, Paul R. Townsend, and in December were recalled to Colorado. Most of the men clamped on their skis, grabbed towing ropes, and were hauled over snowy highways some sixty miles to the railroad station at Lake Louise. Upon return to Camp Hale, they discovered half a dozen Weasels hauled up along the fence next to U.S. Highway 2. Outside, motorists were pulling up to ask questions about these strange new vehicles. The members of the Columbia Icefields Detachment, who had been threatened with court-martial if they made even one vague allusion to the Weasel, listened numbly as the guard happily explained exactly what these vehicles were all about.

Since the division had not been formally activated, it was under the pro tem command of Mountain Training Group, with Colonel Rolfe at the head. By now some hundreds of skiers had been trained in rock climbing and vice versa. The novelty of rock climbing was spreading—helped along, no doubt, by a spectacular demonstration of roped teams using pitons and the most delicate technical methods to climb a cliff to the east of the camp. Lieutenant Charles Bradley, a ski jumper, son of a University of Wisconsin professor, had worked out a little dramatic skit to spice the proceedings. GI clothes and boots were stuffed with straw to create a dummy, not easily discernible as such from a distance. At the very end of the demonstration a real soldier would stage a struggle with the dummy. The latter would finally plunge over the cliff, accompanied by bloodcurdling screams. General McNair watched this demonstration one day. He was not amused.

There followed a rock climbing school for pack artillery officers in Cheyenne Canyon, at Colorado Springs. Large audiences of tourists helped to spread the word that the Army was doing something spectacular. This school climaxed with a luxurious expedition to the snowfields of the Sangre de Cristo Range. The artillery commander, Colonel David L. Ruffner, sent along a whole contingent of cooks and packers to assure the comfort of his officers. Earlier, meanwhile, Jay had taken a small contingent of skiers to Sun Valley for a month, where they were berthed in the best rooms the Challenger Inn had to offer. Another detachment, with much publicity, showed up at Lincoln, New Hampshire, to teach climbing to troops of the 42nd Division. The rumor was assiduously spread that they were training for Norway. The story, however apocryphal, gained currency and was alleged to have caused the diversion of two German divisions to Norway.

The climbing teachers continued to climb while the rest of the division soldiered. A detachment of fifty officers and men was sent to Seneca Rocks, near Elkins, West Virginia, and divisions training for the invasion of France went through a "crash" course in mountaineering two weeks long. They learned, from beginning to end, the techniques of climbing. Who knows how much these thousands of GIs passed on or how much they contributed to the immense growth of American mountaineering after World War II? On night maneuvers, occasionally, they disturbed nesting rattlesnakes, which abounded in the area. One soldier, on a rainy night, heard the warning rattle and then a brushing sensation against his raincoat. When he reached camp he found the puncture marks and venom stains of a rattler. Others, walking through the deep woods in daytime, narrowly escaped stepping on copperheads.

These hazards, uncommon to the battlefield, were not the only ones. The graduation exercise for each group of trainees was an attack on a cliff. Flares of all colors burst overhead as whooping soldiers charged across the headwaters of the Potomac and onto the cliff. The "enemy" detonated dynamite charges and fired blank bullets. But after one charge pulled down a whole section of cliff, the exercise was changed to the daytime hours.

One balmy day, the commanding general of the 77th ("Liberty Bell") Division was standing on the riverbank when a gung-ho soldier leaped in and sank ten feet to the bottom of a pool. The detachment officers stood temporarily stunned, but the general saved the day. "Is that what he's supposed to do?" he asked mildly. At which point, four officers dived in, pulled out the soldier, and revived him.

A week later, on a night exercise, flares started a forest fire it took two days to extinguish.

That same autumn, Lieutenant Benton Thompson, earlier a guide on Mt. Baker, was dispatched to join a combined British-

American detachment at the foot of the Athabaska Glacier, in another section of the Columbia Icefields. He was accompanied by Colonel Wood, an Alaskan explorer, formerly president of the American Alpine Club. And to top it all, a detachment of officers under the aegis of Colonel Avery ("Snowshoe") Cochran was sent to train the Fifth Army in Italy. Their happy days ran out the next spring, when most of them joined the First Special Service force, fighting at Anzio, and then took part in the invasion of southern France.

Only one detachment, five officers and fifteen men dispatched to a joint U.S.-British mountain school in the Apennines, really saw service at high altitude. These men, under the command of Captain H. E. Link, a Seattle ski racer, wound up in a luxurious ski resort at Terminillo, seventy miles from Rome, built by Mussolini. The enlisted men occupied Mussolini's quarters, and hung the dictator's crossed skis on the wall as a memento of the former tenant. The detachment led combat patrols with half a dozen British regiments, including the Household Cavalry, and witnessed the only Allied casualties in Italy caused by an avalanche. Three British soldiers, led by a British major, were crossing a dangerous windslab slope when it broke away. All were dragged and tumbled on their rope 2,000 vertical feet to the valley floor; all were killed by suffocation in the snow.

Yet all this training, though some of it was mildly ridiculous, did establish an American doctrine of mountain climbing—a system for tying safe knots, for handling ropes, for using pitons and for moving fluidly up the most ferocious obstacles. More than that, it established a whole new generation of mountaineering and skiing equipment. Laminated skis, made up of thin glued layers of wood, replaced the old wooden planks with which the 87th started its career, and made turning infinitely easier. Bindings were perfected to be more easily releasable. White felt mukluks, the troops called them "bunny boots," were devised so that soldiers when in camp could forestall frozen feet by transferring from tight leather boots to the looser felt ones. New rucksacks were developed; new, baggy "mountain pants," with huge pockets to carry all the extras a soldier tends to squirrel away.

So were new, lightweight gasoline pressure stoves, cooking kits, and dehydrated rations far superior to the standard Army "K."

These were the work of Bates, Adams Carter and the others who had signed up with the Office of the Quartermaster General to work on special equipment. Perhaps their most important contribution was a combined ski-mountain boot. In the early days, a skier had to wear his ski boots and carry clumsy, nailed boots which worked poorly on rock though well on ice. They had heard reports of a new type of rubber sole, with cleats on it, which mountaineers were using in Europe, called the Bramani sole. "One weekend," recalls Carter, "we were testing equipment at Pinkham Notch Camp, under Mt. Washington, New Hampshire, when a climber walked in with a pair of Bramanis on. We practically wrestled him to the floor, and wouldn't let him up until he promised us those boots. In return, we generously permitted him to complete his climb the next day."

The ski-mountain boot was bulky and heavy, but it could be used for skiing, for rock climbing and for snow and ice. American fork and hoe manufacturers, meanwhile, turned out ice axes by the thousands and pitons by the hundreds of thousands, along with karabiners—snap links through which the rope is passed on a cliffside.

The biggest development, perhaps, was the nylon climbing rope, 120 feet long and 7/16-inch in diameter. Until the war (and in it, so far as the Germans were concerned) manila was the preferred type of rope. But manila strands were short, and manila could break under a sudden fall. Nylon, to the contrary, simply stretched. Division soldiers leaped from "jumping platforms," and sometimes fell as much as forty feet before being brought to a gentle, elongated stop. Mittens, liners for mittens, climbing gloves, special rag socks, special felt insoles for wear in boots during cold weather, crampons with their spiked bottoms for use on ice, new clips for holding rifles firm on rucksacks while a skier was running down the mountain; ultralightweight mountain tents and aluminum shovels—the whole galaxy of equipment required for military mountaineering was provided by the Quartermaster General. Pile-lined parkas and jackets, pile-lined caps, canvas mukluks and new light eiderdown sleeping bags, with zippers guaranteed to open in a hurry if the enemy staged a raid, all these things provided wonderful and practical playthings for a division indoctrinated with the concept of mountain living as the only kind of living.

It was training that made the 10th Mountain Division effective, and it was training that helped English and American troops in Italy overcome a fear of heights, to learn how to move confidently through rough, broken terrain, and to learn how to conserve their energy so they could fight when they hit battle stations.

9

No Japs at All

GEORGE CATLETT MARSHALL, Chief of Staff of the United States Army, was somewhat reverentially regarded by his staff as a man who never made a mistake. That was almost but not quite true. He did make one mistake, in two installments, by sending American troops into the fog, mud and desolation of the wind-blown Aleutian Islands.

The Aleutians stretch westward from the barren Alaska Penin-sula like an erratic dotted line, pointing toward Paramushiro, on the Kurile Islands, where the Japanese in World War II main-tained their northernmost naval base. Viewed on the map, the Aleutians look like natural stepping-stones to Japan and the Asian mainland—or, from the Japanese outlook, like natural step-ping-stones to Alaska and continental North America. In fact, they are perhaps the most intractable islands in the world; snow lies on the ground there nine months of the year. Clammy mist, lashing rains and the keening williwaw winds peculiar to the country around the Bering Sea compound the misery. Fog for days on end lies flat on the water. Given these circumstances, aerial bombing and naval shelling of an enemy would be possi-ble only on rare, clear days.

On June 7, 1942, Japanese forces occupied the islands of Attu and Kiska. Attu was at the very end of the island chain, just 720 miles from Paramushiro; Kiska was 200 miles closer to the Alaskan mainland. The Japanese had no intention of invading Alaska; they simply wanted to make sure that the Americans would not move out the chain from their base at Dutch Harbor, yet another thousand miles to the west. Also, as they correctly surmised, the American public would react with anger and concern. The outcry was particularly loud in the Pacific Northwest, where newspapers and uninformed citizens feared the Japanese would move from the Aleutians to Alaska and then down through the trackless Coast Ranges of British Columbia, finally staging a victory parade into Seattle.

This concern was reflected in Washington, where the very presence of Japanese troops on American soil—wet, spongy and hostile though that soil might be—was regarded as an insult not to be overlooked. The mistake of reacting to the Japanese gesture was not George Marshall's alone. His colleagues of the Joint Chiefs of Staff, Admirals Ernest R. King and William D. Leahy, agreed with him that the Japanese had to be routed. Subsequent American moves were like a comedy of errors—not so comic on Attu, where United States losses were heavy, but a wry *opera bouffe* on Kiska. It is hard to tell who profited least from the struggle over the Aleutians. The Japanese forces on Attu and Kiska, numbering 10,583 men, might have turned the tide at Guadalcanal. The 41,000 Americans and Canadians used to invade those islands could have appreciably shortened the time-span of General Douglas MacArthur's island-hopping campaign in the South Pacific.

The Attu invasion force not only was badly led, trained for desert warfare, but was also badly equipped. The troops wore the standard leather GI combat boot, which soaked through in minutes. About a third of the 41,000 invaders succumbed to trench foot, a crippling disability caused by wearing wet boots for days on end without even a change of socks. The Army Quartermaster Corps was already stockpiling shoe pacs, with rubber to the ankle and leather tops, and had issued them to the 87th Mountain Infantry Regiment, but somebody along the line forgot to provide them to the 7th Infantry Division before it landed on Attu. Totally green, psychologically unprepared for this land of booming surf and howling winds, the soldiers of the division came ashore under the worst possible handicaps. The result was predictable: utter chaos.

The 7th landed May 11, 1943, when wet snow still lay on the ground. Opposing them were only 2,400 Japanese, who wisely retreated to a high mountain pass defensible from both sides. Groping through fog, wallowing in snow while bulldozers and trucks bogged down in the underlying mud, it took the Americans 18 days to complete their mission on an island only 15 miles wide. The apprehensive Army commander, Major General A. E. Brown, moved his troops forward only 4,800 yards in 48 hours. He frantically called for reinforcements, and was heard to predict that it would take him six months to invest the island. The peppery expedition commander, Admiral Thomas C. Kinkaid, replaced him with a tougher fighter, Major General Eugene Landrum. On May 29, with an American victory in sight, a thousand howling Japanese staged a banzai charge. When stopped by American soldiers, 500 of them committed suicide with hand grenades, and the other 500 were killed by United States fire.

"I should have sent Alpine troops to Attu," Marshall confessed to Dole some months later. He did send Alpine troops to Kiska in August, not only the 87th but also the mountain-trained First Special Service Force, plus some 5,300 Canadians, a battalion of Marines, and three "flatland" U.S. Army regiments, in all a total of 34,426 soldiers. Technically Kiska wasn't Alpine terrain, though Kiska Volcano rises 4,000 feet from the sea. But it was terrain that required tough, sure-footed men conditioned to extremes of weather, as the 87th had been conditioned on Mt. Rainier and in a bitter, subzero winter at Camp Hale.

While the Americans were compounding their original error, assembling a huge task force at Fort Ord, California, the Japanese were admitting their mistake in going into the Aleutians at all. But they didn't tell Washington. They decided to pull out of Kiska, leaving it to the sea lions, the seals, and a couple of mongrel dogs, pets of the garrison.

Under cover of fog and churning seas, 600 men of the occupation force were evacuated by seven "I" class submarines between May 27 and June 21. On July 28, the Tokyo Express arrived—a force of light cruisers and destroyers. In 55 minutes, the remaining 5,183 men of the garrison were hustled aboard. Weather and American bungling, to quote the great naval historian Samuel Eliot Morison, were responsible for the Japanese success. Fog screened the Tokyo Express from American bomber patrols; blockading American destroyers were off duty that day.

The American invasion force could not have been more formidable. Rear Admiral F. W. Rockwell commanded nearly a hundred ships. The troops were equipped with rubber suits for protection from the rain, shoe pacs, sleeping bags and winter clothing. The invasion itself was regarded as so important that John J. McCloy, Assistant Secretary of War, came along to observe the American fighting man as he avenged Pearl Harbor. Soldiers were briefed and rebriefed on shipboard. "I wanted to go ashore after the troops had landed," recalls McCloy, but the admirals and generals said, "Oh, no. It's too dangerous. We don't know how many Japs are still around." The theme was that the tricky Japs were capable of any atrocity, that they were supermen so polished in the art of murder that a soldier really needed eyes in the back of his head. What this vivid language did was to scare the pants off most of the invaders, none of whom had ever before been blooded in battle. Major Emmet L. Nations, a battalion commander in the 87th, immortalized himself in song and story when, in a speech that ought to have been titled "Destination, Kiska," he announced to his assembled troops: "This is it, men! Can you hear me in the rear?"

In retrospect, the armed forces should have known there were no Japanese left on Kiska. Naval forces had blasted the Japanese installations without receiving one round of counterfire; Air Corps and Navy planes were over early and late, bombing Kiska through overcast and strafing the garrison areas when the weather permitted low-level flights. A photo mission flown August 2, revealed twenty-six buildings destroyed and all but one of twenty barges sunk in the harbor. But there were some nagging questions, never answered.

Why had the Japanese bunched up their trucks in the motor pool near Kiska Harbor instead of dispersing them for protection? Why had Radio Kiska gone off the air July 28 and never come on again? Why did coast defense guns fail to fire on American warships or antiaircraft fail to fire on American planes? Yet spotters for one air strike reported light flak, some fliers said they saw tracer bullets, and one pilot insisted he had strafed a fleeing Japanese, who fell flat. The high command concluded that the perfidious enemy was simply in hiding, waiting to annihilate the Americans when they set foot on shore.

Not all the young gentlemen of the 87th were overawed by the thought of the invasion. As the U.S.S. *Zeilin* cruised toward Kiska, deep in the hold, Private Dino Sonnino, son of a former Foreign Minister of Italy, was loudly reading Dante and the *Decameron* to his platoon mates, translating it from Latin to English in a booming voice. The platoon sergeant, Alfons Waverek, regarded as the toughest soldier around, listened with some bemusement and then burst out: "You guys! Here some of us may be gettin' killed, and you're readin' poetry!"

On the transport *Harris*, Second Lieutenant Livermore was busy maintaining his diary. In it, he noted with some astonishment his conversation with a soldier who shared deck duty. "He was a clean-cut young man," he observed, but the clean-cut young man regaled Livermore with an account of his career as a pimp in an eastern mill town. The incident illuminates the whole character of the 87th and, subsequently, the whole 10th Mountain Division—college graduates and roughnecks; millionaires and mule skinners; foresters and sportsmen; farm boys and successful businessmen who suspended their careers because they believed in the concept of an Alpine fighting force.

Livermore, as befits a scholarly New Englander, was as much interested in natural history as in his troops. "Have seen," he wrote in his diary, "a bald eagle, a black and russet-cheeked sparrow, ravens wheeling, and gulls and puffins. . . . The boys are head in the clouds, itching to go."

His diary continued:

"D-day was called the 15th of August at 0635 Yellow and Blue Beaches, on the western side of Kiska. [Chosen for purposes of surprise, these beaches were opposite Kiska Harbor, to deceive the nonexistent Japanese.] Turned in about 7 the night before, just as in preparation for a big ski race, everyone a mixture of unnatural calmness, nervous laughter, and still unfinished business bustle. Reveille at midnight with sandwiches and coffee, final packing of the battle packs (poncho, Sterno and socks) stowing away 136 rounds of armor, four grenades and a K ration. First wave into the boats at 3 A.M. with Kiska about five miles off the starboard bow as we headed north.

"It looked very quiet, very steep, very, very ominous. The sea was calm, clouds about a hundred feet above us, and the moon shining through breaks like the sun on the plains when there are thunderstorms scattered about. I remember praying that the moon would stay off our boats, that the offshore breeze would keep the sound of engines away from Jap outposts' ears, and just praying! Haven't prayed that earnestly in a long time. Remember the sergeant saying after we landed, 'A lot of atheists were converted this morning.' "

In K Company Second Lieutenant Roger Eddy, son of a distinguished Connecticut family, was considerably less gung-ho. Two days out from San Francisco, the company commander collapsed and had to be transferred to the hospital. The 3rd Battalion commander, Lieutenant Colonel George Henderson, summoned Eddy to his stateroom and said, "Eddy, I'm promoting you to captain and making you company commander." For a shavetail to be jumped two grades was unique, and Eddy cherished the honor, but not for long. Before he got off Kiska, a letter came through from the War Department revoking his captaincy and reducing him to first lieutenant. The Adjutant General's office observed that nobody could jump two ranks. General Custer, the letter pointed out, did jump from second lieutenant to brigadier general, but that was a clerical error.

To Eddy, the night of the invasion was a night of horror. Rangers had been sent ashore to spy out the Japanese positions. They were supposed to report what they had found, but since they found nothing, they went on through the fog to the eastern shore of the island without sending back a single message. When the 3rd Battalion got ashore, in a chaotic mess, it was generally assumed the Rangers hadn't reported because they were locked in battle.

K Company took up a position on a hill overlooking Gertrude Cove, one of the landing beaches. "There was a lot of rifle fire," Eddy recalls. "Every time a helmet poked up through the fog everyone let go, and a lot of people simply fired because they thought they saw Japs in the murk. We were all scared stiff; we were green; and everybody expected to die.

"The Army had issued us field radios, but they hadn't told us how to use them, so I thought I'd go out and check on the position of the other companies. While I was making my rounds, I heard the rumor that the Japs had been driven down toward Kiska Harbor and were still somewhere out in the fog. Then one of my machine gunners cut loose with a whole string of bullets. He'd heard there were Japs down in the draw to our right. As a matter of fact, he was firing on our own battalion headquarters. Battalion in turn phoned regimental headquarters, 'We're surrounded. Send help.' And then everyone started shooting."

The I Company commander sent out the platoons of Second Lieutenants William Hamill and Wilfred J. Funk to repel the attack. They were killed in the melee, along with three enlisted men, and Second Lieutenant Dave Harris, son of a New York broker, was shot in the knee. Funk was the grandson of the lexicographer and the son of the president of Funk and Wagnalls, book and dictionary publishers. Corporal Richard Rocker, formerly a junior executive with the New York Telephone Company, was high on a hill with I Company when the shooting started. "I could hear one poor devil grunt as he was hit by a bullet," Rocker recalls, "and then his body came tumbling down the hill past me." A little later, there was a cry from M Company, in the valley below: "We've got a Jap infiltrator in among us!" and the shooting redoubled.

"Funk was," says Eddy, "the original hero type—clean-cut, enthusiastic, intelligent. It was a tragedy he had to die because we all had panicked. I lost men of my own in that miserable skirmish. I can remember bending over one of my sergeants who had been shot between the eyes. And while I was looking at him, he died.

"The next morning, when we realized what had happened, we felt as if we'd been on an all-night drunk. We were exhausted, disgusted, and ashamed. And we knew we'd done all the killing ourselves." The lesson was a hard one to learn, but Eddy benefitted from it, becoming one of the best combat officers in the 10th Mountain Division.

That was a wild first night on Kiska, with some wryly funny events to counterbalance the tragedy of I and K Companies. In B Company Second Lieutenant John Clement encountered a Harvard classmate, Second Lieutenant William C. McGuckin. "Come on, McGuckin," he said, "get that rendezvous-with-death look off your face." In L Company, Private First Class Murray de Camp Spear, a New York insurance man and a veteran amateur skier, earned himself a Purple Heart in the war that wasn't. Spear, like many of the soldiers of the 87th, was in his thirties, and therefore able to review the Battle of Kiska with some dispassionateness.

"They had us terrified before we landed," Spear said. "The whole theme was the Mysterious Orient and the Inscrutable Jap: They were going to wait until we all were ashore and then pounce on us. When we got ashore and didn't find any Japs, the scuttlebutt was that they were hiding in the crater of Kiska Volcano, ready to dash down and bayonet us. And then with all that, there was rain, mist, and a penetrating, nasty, thirty-five to forty mile an hour wind that actually drove a couple of the men out of their minds.

"We finally dug in atop a hill. We were certain we had to stay awake or the Japs would kill all of us. Every time a figure was dimly visible, somebody would let off a few rounds or throw a concussion grenade. My carbine jammed, and all I had was a GI hunting knife. I figured I'd be bayoneted any minute. Just a little distance away was my sergeant, Clyde Limoges, with his messenger, John Lonnaissen. 'Sarge,' I yelled over. 'I'm unarmed and I'm scared. I want to come over to be with you.' 'Come ahead,' yelled Limoges. I came bounding over, leaped into the foxhole, and Lonnaissen shot me in the groin. He'd been asleep, and he thought I was a Jap. They bandaged me, and I was evacuated to Adak."

Since Kiska was technically a theater of war, even *sans* Japanese, Spear's company commander wrote out a glowing recommendation, and the base commander at Adak handed him a Purple Heart. That wasn't the end of it. Invalided out of the 87th, he was in officer candidate school, Transportation Corps, when World War II came to an end. The school commander was determined that any heroes within his jurisdiction would not be overlooked. Unaware that Spear already had one Purple Heart, he called him before the assembled cadets, praised the example of bravery he had set, and awarded him a second Purple Heart. Spear considers he probably is the only GI who was twice honored for being shot by one of his friends in a military engagement where only friendly troops were involved.

Livermore's platoon had come ashore unopposed: "Not a shot, not a sign of struggle, just quiet figures scattered all over the slopes, apparently moving in slow motion like cold ants. . . . There followed one of the most miserable and increasingly bitter days and nights I ever hope to endure. With tales of snipers and Jap patrols seen dimly through the clouds by our predecessors, the men were alert beyond all expectations, but the driving wind and soaking clouds wet us to the skin.

"I still remember jokes and cussing, with an irrepressible urge on almost everyone's part to get going after the Japs at all costs. Walking around on the bare dome of Larry Hill against a fifty-mile windswept fog, I remember a soldier named Pell saying to his foxhole companion: 'Boy, I'll get me a Jap and cook his kidneys!' To which the question: 'How 'n hell do you cook Jap kidneys?' Grimly, 'Boil the piss out'n them.'

"I remember Father John Bracken, the Catholic chaplain, cheering us around a drizzly campfire with his idea of how he would recall these days on Kiska in later life—that future life we all dream of as civilians again. His formula: 'I shall lie in a bathtub of cold water, naked except for a poncho, with a fan trained on me from above, and have someone to toss C biscuits at me every three hours!'

"Already the watchwords of the Kiska trip are being born— just little sayings that will forever remain in all our minds:

" 'I know you'll like your mission. I know it and I like it. When you know it as I do, I know you'll like it too! It's an appropriate mission. Now, remember to change your socks when they get wet and carry extras in your shirt!' which was Lieutenant Colonel Jeff Willis' speech at Ford Ord before the 87th shoved off.

" 'Forty thousand men, five battleships, and *one* dead Jap!' The dead Jap being one found dead by the 3rd Battalion, of natural causes in a mountain shelter.

"In our foxhole we recalled these and invented more, even launching ourselves on a fanciful punishment for striking defense workers labeled, 'The Foxhole Purge.' It envisioned such strikers being forced to live in foxholes outside the factory with hoses rigged up to provide sufficient water, airplane motors to create wind, K rations thrown at them, Sterno without matches—in fact all we could imagine even approaching our own plight.

"When we next received orders from Battalion we were told to police up that damned cliff where E and G Companies had been living for a week. This would have seemed the last straw until Sergeant Rudy Konieczny laughed and said, 'When I get home and my children ask: What did you do in the war, Daddy, I'll say that I policed up Kiska, son.' " Konieczny, a champion ski racer from western Massachusetts, was later killed in Italy.

The snafu continued apace after the discovery that the Japanese had gone. Barracks bags, twenty deep, covered half an acre of swampy tundra, and many soldiers never reclaimed their belongings, including the cherished eiderdown sleeping bags. Mail delivery was so slow that Corporal Lee Glidden, of the paint family, pulled down his cap, pulled up his collar, went to the mail tent, introduced himself as "Colonel Greene," and brusquely demanded the mail for the 2nd Battalion.

Glidden, a prolific letter writer, ran contrary to regulations once too often. Soldiers had been ordered to send back no information about Japanese defensive works. Glidden blithely dispatched several letters with accurate drawings of fortifications on the island. The censors opened these letters, and Glidden was tossed into the brig. But lo! Several weeks later he was released and ordered to Infantry Officer Candidate School, for which he had applied before he was dispatched to Kiska.

Kiska was a dull place to be, but the 87th included so many college glee club (or drinking club) singers that it spawned one of the regiment's most popular songs, music from "The Battle Hymn of the Republic," words original:

> *The 87th Mountain Infantry went out to hunt some Japs,*
> *To add another feather to their khaki Mountain caps.*
> *We kissed the Golden Gate goodbye, and didn't moan*
>   *perhaps—*
> *But we didn't get a God Dam Sonofabitch of a Jap!*
> CHORUS:
> *All we ever got was Kiska [3 times]*
> *But we didn't get a God Dam Sonofabitch of a Jap!*

. . . and so on, for five more verses.

A more sardonic set of lyrics, six verses long, was sung to the tune of that lilting barroom ballad "No Balls at All." A sample verse and the chorus went:

> *We headed for Kiska with blood in our eye,*
> *But G-2 had told us a hell of a lie!*
> *10,000 Japs soldiers were due for a fall—*
> *But when we got there, there were no Japs at all!*
> CHORUS:
> *What! No Japs at all? Yes, no Japs at all—*
> *A very small island with no Japs at all.*

We learned how to stay out in any ol' clime.
We jumped on our skis when they gave us the call—
Then came to an island with no Japs at all!

The 87th left Kiska by driblets, the final contingent not until January 1944. To punctuate the boredom, practically everyone scaled Kiska volcano. One college graduate completed a thesis on the flora and fauna of Kiska that won him a Ph.D. Others adopted Aleutian blue foxes, so unaccustomed to man they could be trained as pets. Bob Livermore wrote home: "All I could think to tell my tent mates at night was: 'Set the alarm and put the fox out.'" Hand grenades stunned or killed spawning salmon to provide fresh fish dinners, much to the scandal of the fly fishermen in the regiment. Stovepipes were cleaned by dropping in a sack of powder, an operation that sometimes took the tent with it. Artillery shells were hammered into the ground to serve as tent pegs. A colonel from headquarters, visiting one platoon area, gave the lieutenant in charge a dressing down for placing his tents so close to an artillery dump. While the lieutenant was standing at attention, the colonel noticed two men taking shells from the dump. His eyes widened as he realized what they were doing. They were using the shells for pegs. Without a word the colonel jumped into his jeep and drove hastily away.

And then there were scores of other little incidents. One stormy night all but one pyramidal tent in Headquarters Company blew down. The survivors, including the regimental sergeant major, huddled into a single tent and secured it to a T-15 snow jeep. At dawn a corporal braved the storm to start his vehicle. When he drove away the tent went with him, leaving sleeping officers and men exposed to a downpour of rain.

That was Kiska—as primitive, says Roger Eddy, as if God had just created it—where now and then the clouds would part to reveal a snowy volcano somewhere far off in the distant Pacific and then roll back again. That was Kiska, and the 87th left it without regret to the blue foxes, the puffins and the roaring sea lions.

10

Of Men and Mules

"THROUGH THESE PORTALS," read a sign over the corral at North Fort Lewis, Washington, "pass the most beautiful mules in the world." It was a paraphrase of the sign Sherman Billingsley installed over the doorway of the Stork Club, in New York, only he was talking about girls, not mules. To the skiers who had joined the mountain troops, the mules were at once a horror and a challenge: a horror because the big Army mule is the most stealthy and dangerous adversary any peacetime soldier could face; a challenge to see if the critter could be outwitted. Mules are shrewd animals. They will wait for days until an unwary man strays within range of their hind legs, and then lash out with a crippling kick. If they are overloaded, they simply lie down and refuse to move. If they are feeling jaundiced, they puff out their bellies, making it almost impossible to cinch the straps that hold the carrying saddle. But they can carry up to 320 pounds for miles on end, and they are notably phlegmatic. A horse will flinch at a shadow; a mule will plod through an artillery barrage as if it never existed.

The Army mules were huge, brawny fellows reared at the Remount Depot at Fort Reno, Oklahoma. Each battalion had a hundred of them, along with farm boys from the South who could teach neophytes how to handle them. These youngsters were homesick; the mules were their only friends. At the beginning, duty officers checking the barracks would find half a dozen men absent from each. Where they slept was, for a time, a mystery. Then a resourceful officer made a check of the stables. Here were the mule men, not sleeping in the stalls, but sleeping just outside them, as close to their friends as might be safe. By the time the 10th Mountain Division was completely organized at Camp Hale, close to 5,000 mules had been attached. Of these, some 3,200 were in four pack artillery battalions—the 604th, 614th, 615th and 616th. Each battalion transported eight 75-millimeter pack howitzers, the same little guns the American Army and its mule battalions had used in France in World War I. Each howitzer was broken into six pieces. The mule artillery-men could slap them together and commence firing within five minutes. Mule stories were legion. At Jolon, during maneuvers in California, one mule tumbled end over end down a precipitous hill and was covered with dripping scarlet when he finally came to rest. Appalled soldiers, rushing down to see if the animal were mortally wounded, discovered that he was carrying the maneuver force's entire supply of bottled catsup. Colonel Rolfe, inspecting the stables at Fort Lewis one day, was startled to see a husky blacksmith haul off and hit a mule so hard between the eyes that the animal reeled. "Son," he said reprovingly, "that's no way to treat an animal." The blacksmith shrugged. "Maybe so, colonel," he said, "but the son of a bitch is standing on my foot." By the time all the mules had joined the division, the college graduates were as good at handling them as the mule skinners.

It took the command a long time to realize that mountain men afoot could move more effectively in the hills than mountain men on horseback. At Fort Lewis, all officers were required to take equitation—training in riding. There was some suspicion that Rolfe, an old cavalryman, was exacting revenge for the figure he cut, understandably, as a floundering beginner on skis. Officers who came to ski but had to ride were thrown with monotonous regularity. They were required to write down the reason in a log book at the stables. Lieutenant John C. Jay, a notably good skier, won the prize for the most apt remark. "Caught an edge," he wrote. Catching an edge while skiing is almost a certain prelude to a fall. The equitation classes eventually vanished, but not the Army's infatuation with men on horseback as a means of reconnaissance. However, after several disastrous experiences, the 10th Cavalry Reconnaissance Troop lost its horses. The officers were transferred out, and the new officers all were rock climbers and skiers, sporting the rare and prestigious cavalry sabers. Two of the officers who went to Italy to serve with the British Army were wearing these sabers on the plane that took the detachment from Brazil across the South Atlantic to Dakar in West Africa. A Cavalry colonel, complete with walrus moustache and crossed sabers on his lapels, almost wept when he saw the familiar insignia. When he learned that these cavalrymen were mountain climbers, he retired to his seat on the plane and remained there, muttering, for most of the long trip.

Through 1942 and 1943 the future division went through a series of dizzying mutations. A Norwegian battalion, the 90th, was attached and then detached for assumed combat service in Norway. The 87th Mountain Infantry was completely activated, with three battalions, June 1, 1942, and on December 6, 1942, the regiment moved—mules and all—to Camp Hale. The 86th Mountain Infantry was activated in the spring of 1943, but a formally organized division still remained to be set up. A provisional command under Rolfe, by now a brigadier general, carried the title of "Mountain Training Center" and then "Mountain Training Group." First recruits for the 85th Mountain Infantry were flowing in before the 10th Light Division was created—not to become the 10th Mountain Division until almost the moment for shipment overseas.

Camp Hale, it developed, was almost an unmitigated disaster. It had never occurred to the Pentagon that this isolated camp, in a barren pocket among the high Colorado hills, was at too high an altitude, 9,000 feet. Most Alpine passes, at their highest point, range from 6,000 to 8,000 feet. The altitude of Hale was about the same as that of the Hörnli hut, where the final ascent of the Matterhorn takes place. The camp was also in a far drier climate, really a high semidesert, where trees grew only because of moisture from Pacific Ocean storms, lofted across the projecting Rockies. The results were unpleasant.

"Troopers began developing a rasping cough," Jay later wrote, in a history of the Mountain Training Center. "It was known as the 'Pando hack,' named for the whistle-stop station at Camp Hale, "a cough that shook the whole frame and left the cougher weak and watery-eyed." The strenuous life at so high an altitude, when the lungs demand maximum oxygen, sharpened tempers and wore men out physically. Hundreds developed respiratory problems or heart murmurs and had to be sent to lower-altitude divisions. Then there was the soot that hung like a lowering cloud over the encampment. The clean, white snows of skiing song and story were there, all right, but they were high above the camp. Barracks stoves burned lignite coal, and more than 500 smokestacks discharged its greasy effluent. Protected from wind, the camp was in shadow even when the sun was brightest. Whenever a little breeze did manage to dispel the cloud, loud whistling would announce the advent of heavy freight trains, each with three snorting locomotives, each locomotive sending up its own contributory smoke. Pando had a four percent gradient, one of the steepest in the country, and it took those three smoky locomotives to push the trains westward, up over the Continental Divide, into Leadville.

A letter from a California recruit, written January 26, 1943, spelled out the misery: "I believe the perpetual smoke cloud, train smoke and all the soft coal smoke from all the buildings here that hangs like a pall over the camp, night and day, is in part, at least, responsible for this darn business. This morning, on my way up here to the Orderly Room, I could just make out the outline of the 8th barracks building 50 feet away, and every breath I took just reeked of the smoke.

"For the first time, last night, it was so thick in the barracks itself that you could plainly see it by looking at the light at the end of the room, and two of the fellows coughed so much that they couldn't take it and both left for the show. C—— was mad as a hornet; he paced up and down swearing like I've never heard him before and finally went upstairs into one of the corporals' private rooms, locked the door and windows and the heat vent, and didn't come out for three hours."

The disenchantment with Camp Hale was sharpest among the 80 percent of soldiers who had not asked to be sent there. Half the men of the 110th Signal Company, solidly southern, had to be shipped out. In fact, until late spring 1943, most of the troops staffing the Mountain Training Center came from the 31st (Dixie) Division at Leesville, Louisiana, in Jay's words one of the hottest, lowest, flattest spots in the whole United States. Others were transferred from the 33rd Division at Camp Forrest, Tennessee, and the 30th at Memphis. They hated the snow, they hated the camp, and they had a particularly venomous hate for their skis. "Mah to-chuah (torture) boards," was a popular southern phrase. The hatred extended even as high as Sergeant Major Jones, no southerner he. After a winter of pratfalls at Mt. Rainier, he chopped his skis into tiny pieces and fed them into a fire.

The Army in its blind majesty even dispatched a company of Mexican-Americans, fresh from desert training. Colonel Cook, roused from sleep on a 30-below-zero night to go down to the station, found them shivering in suntans on the platform. After hastily arranging heated housing, he called II Corps Headquarters in Memphis and irately insisted they be moved to some other camp, as they were. For the former flatland soldiers, Hale, to many recruits, was known as Camp Hell. Everyone was restricted to post for ten days running. Leadville, the only nearby town, was off limits most of the time as obliging young ladies flocked in from less profitable beats elsewhere in the Rockies. Denver, by way of the Royal Gorge Route, was a nine-hour trip. Lucky soldiers with cars made the trip in about four and a half hours, and charged staggering prices for passengers. USO troupes, fearful of the altitude, shunned the place. The service clubs offered nothing stronger than 3.2 beer, but even this watery substitute for the real thing was enough to stir disgruntled mule skinners to action against "them skiers."

In the middle of a blizzard, the duty officer was routed from bed to receive an entire Pigeon Platoon. It subsequently developed that most of the pigeons could not fly at 10,000-feet altitude. They could only walk, carrying their dispatches afoot like a Western Union messenger, and were subsequently dispatched to warmer and lower Army bases to carry out their mission.

The basic trouble at Camp Hale was that the Army knew only on the most general basis what mountain troops ought to be doing, and the senior commanders were ignorant of mountain problems. Some reserve and regular officers marched their troops at 110 paces per minute and couldn't understand—until the doctors told them—why so many men fell out. One battalion executive announced to a detachment of mostly green troops from flat country that "Anywhere my dog can climb, you can climb," and relented only when faced by revolt. In ski school the real commanders were ex-teachers such as Sergeant Peter Gabriel and Sergeant Olaf Rodegard, of Mt. Hood. Colonels scrambled to obey their orders. In rock climbing school, where failure to pay attention to business could lead to a broken neck, privates and corporals schooled in the Alps and Rockies were downright peremptory to their superiors.

Kay Boyle, who brought along her three small von Franckenstein children, found herself quarters in the optimistically named Palace Hotel at Leadville and spent the winter of 1942 in an atmosphere of unrelieved cold and gloom. "The whole experience," she said later, "was simply dreadful, even if I did see George perhaps once in every two weeks when they let him off post for a weekend." She did, however, minimize the boredom by writing *His Human Majesty,* a novel with Camp Hale as the setting, the only literate work about the ski troops in wartime. Thereafter, she moved to more civilized quarters in Denver. In 1944, wearying of the bumbling and fumbling at Hale, von Franckenstein transferred to the OSS, signed up as a ski teacher with the mountain troops in the Tyrol, mimicked the peasant accent so accurately he was accepted at face value, and was on hand to greet Patton's troops when they came through Innsbruck to seal the Brenner Pass.

The same Camp Hale malaise affected First Lieutenant William Farnsworth Loomis of the Medical Corps. He transferred to OSS and, while in Washington, decided to pay a social call on "Cousin Harry" to explain why. "Cousin Harry" was Henry L. Stimson, a second cousin once removed. "I told him I was sick of taking part in training which consisted of freezing and frightening men so that they couldn't learn anything," recalls Loomis. "In a very tired voice, he said to me, 'I wish you fellows would stop joining up with glamour outfits and, instead, sign up with a regular division and get this war over.'" If Stimson any longer had a special interest in the mountain troops, he did not reveal it to his young cousin.

Meanwhile, green troops by the hundreds were shipped in to Camp Hale for basic training on three to four feet of snow and at temperatures mainly ranging from zero down. All the simple little things like firing for record on the rifle range became immensely complicated. When ski instruction was piled atop the normal basic routine, it nearly killed the newcomers. Along with this came some opera-bouffe training in the Manual of Skis, a wintry substitute for the Manual of Arms with a rifle. The movements, when carried out with six-foot skis, produced dull thuds and earnest cursing from those in the rear ranks who were clobbered. New men were sent out on maneuvers after only a few hours of instruction. Most were too exhausted to do battle, even mock battle, after reaching their objective. I can recall stopping to watch the commander of A Company 87th attempting to teach the snowplow to half a dozen recruits who could not even stand up on their skis. "Gotta get 'em up the mountain," he explained. "Got a company maneuver up there."

There are no glaciers in Colorado except the vestigial tongue of year-round snow known as St. Mary's Glacier near Georgetown. Colorado snow falls as powder, compacts, and then melts under the late March sun. So the Engineers built a glacier in the valley of nearby Resolution Creek. Logs were piled on a steep slope to create simulated seracs and crevasses, and then water was poured over them. The result was an ice cliff, on which the use of crampons, ropes, ice-axes and ice pitons could be taught. The trouble was that Colorado ice was like no glacier ice anywhere else—unyielding, hard to chop. Also, the glacier didn't last long. Built in early spring, on a sound slope, it melted under the implacable sun.

A second glacier, built hastily on a shady north slope, lasted until mid-May, but with all the delays only a fraction of the troops ever learned much about snow and ice climbing.

In the vast confusion of Camp Hale, everybody tried everything. Fierce sentry dogs were imported, managing to bite a number of their masters. Messenger dogs did better; they could travel over the snow faster than a man. But since it took fifty men to handle twenty dogs, the whole experiment was discarded as wasteful of fighting power. Sled dogs seemed a little more romantic, but they were a lot less practical, since they could travel only on packed trails. The only practical alternative, in the end, was for each soldier to carry everything he needed in his own bulging pack.

The mules met Waterloo on a forty-five-mile trip over the mountains to Aspen, in November 1942. Everything was roses on the way over, but when it came time to go back to Hale, things had changed. Sent off by all the seven hundred citizens of Aspen and a brass band, the expedition ran into drifts thirty feet high and a cornice only skiers could cross. The men and mules turned back to Aspen, and went home to Hale by truck. Ben Thompson, then a corporal, was the man who made the decision. "We could get over," he explained, "but the mules couldn't. We would have lost them all."

Glamorous to the outside world—John Jay had made a film showing mountain troopers skimming down the slopes—disgruntled among themselves, a favorite wisecrack was: "Anyone who transfers to combat from the mountain troops is yellow!" A day of reckoning at Camp Hale was certain to come. Come it did between February 4 and 12, 1943, when a reinforced detachment of a thousand men from the 87th, plus a battalion of pack artillery, was dispatched on maneuvers under the peak of 13,500-foot Homestake Mountain, a few miles from Hale. It was the wildest, coldest time of winter. Blizzards blew in sheets across the high timber through which the detachment had to climb to reach its positions. Colonel Avery Cochran, the G–3 of Mountain Training Center, was known as "Snowshoe Cochran" to his officers. He despised skis, admired snowshoes, and was convinced that machinery could solve every problem of oversnow travel. The maneuver proved Cochran a flop.

Nobody had told the men to wax skis for the long climb up to Homestake, or to use the plush climbing skins with which each soldier was equipped. Men stood freezing outside for two hours before being given the order to march. Once on the packed trail to the bivouac area, all except the most experienced spent most of their time sliding backward and falling. Weighted down with 84- to 90-pound packs, dozens struggled futilely to get up once they had fallen. A march pace of 106 steps a minute was ordered, and nobody could maintain it in the thin atmosphere. The heavy packs compressed lungs so that movement was painful. Some were new recruits with only a few days of ski training. They hadn't been told how to protect themselves from the cold, or even how to operate the ingenious little aluminum mountain gasoline stoves the Quartermaster General's office had developed. Many had to eat their dehydrated rations cold.

First Sergeant Leslie J. Hurley of B Company recalls the whole exercise as sheer agony. One after another his men from B company melted away over the next several days, going back to camp and heated barracks. In other companies men pulled off their boots and exposed their bare feet. "I'd damn well rather have frostbite than stay up in this hell," one soldier said. The maneuver was a fiasco. The "enemy detail," which the 87th was, never needed to go into action. The only useful demonstration of the lethal power of mountains was supplied by the Pack Artillery. Rolfe, according to Major Walter Wood, sent on from Washington as an observer, ordered out a platoon to pick up some parachute supplies which were dropped on a steep slope overlooking Homestake Lake. "Don't!" begged Wood. "That's an

avalanche slope." While the argument was going on, Colonel
David L. Ruffner, the artillery commander, decided to fire a few
shells into the slope to see if he could dislodge it. After half a
dozen rounds, he brought down an immense avalanche that
smashed the ice on the lake and pushed most of the water out
of it.

Fortunately for the future of the mountain troops, there were
important observers present. Army Ground Forces had dispatched Dole, Major Walter A. Wood, Captain Tappin and
William P. House, a member of the first American expedition to
K2 in the Himalayas. When House found Colonel Cochran snug
in a pyramidal tent while his men froze and fell outside, he let
loose with a fierce tongue-lashing.

"The Retreat from Moscow," as the maneuver came to be
known, was the subject of a blistering report to General Mc-
Nair's office. In this retreat 260 men, or about 30 percent of the
command, were invalided out by frostbite or simple exhaustion.
On March 11, 1943, McNair wrote the following report to General Rolfe:

1. Recent observations of activities of your command made by members of this headquarters are forwarded for your information and such
action as you desire.

2. a. The winter training did not appear to be adequate to condition personnel for marching and maneuvering under conditions of extreme cold and adverse winter weather conditions.

b. Members of units did not appear to have had sufficient instruction in the use of special winter clothing and equipment to obtain the
maximum value of their characteristics.

c. March discipline of units appeared slack. A high percentage of
the personnel fell out due to sickness, fatigue, frostbite, and fear.

d. Men were overloaded to such an extent as to reduce mobility
to a minimum and cause unnecessary fatigue and hardship.

e. In bivouac, uniformity of snow camping technique was lacking,
indicating a lack of preliminary instruction.

f. Training programs indicated a lack of planning to provide frequent overnight exercises necessary to properly condition men for winter maneuvers of extended duration.

g. Morale seemed lower than should be expected due to an ab-
normally high morbidity rate attributed to:

(1) Smoke pall
(2) Altitude
(3) Lack of recreational facilities
(4) Lack of confidence in training program

h. The large proportion of experienced woodsmen, mountaineers, guides and trappers in the enlisted and lower commissioned grades provides an excellent source of technical knowledge. This source should be used to the utmost in the development of instructional training technique which is founded on time-tested mountain and winter procedures.

i. Individual prejudice and theories appeared to have biased many decisions of the Mountain and Winter Warfare Board. Fair comparison had not been used in testing equipment and developing techniques.

j. Insufficient liaison existed between the Air Force unit conducting air supply tests and officers of your staff. The result was an incomplete understanding of mutual problems and limitations in supply by air.

k. Artillery firing conducted under difficult conditions was excellent.

3. It is recognized by this headquarters that your command has recently undergone a large expansion and that the entire project is in a continuous state of development, and expansion. The comments in this letter are offered constructively. This headquarters stands ready to assist in remedial action of any matters beyond your control.

Wood, in a separate report, observed that the average load the mountain soldier had to carry was enough to render him worthless for battle. There were 52 items totaling 84 pounds 4 ounces, but in some cases special equipment brought the load up to a stupefying 100 pounds, even more than the "Ninety Pounds of Rucksack" immortalized in the regimental song. In addition to essential items such as sleeping bag, M–1 rifle and ammunition in a belt, the load included such peripheral things as mukluks, a brush, handkerchiefs, emergency snowshoes, entrenching tools, a match box and wristlets. All in their way and at the right time might have been essential, but a good many of them could have been carried up the mountain by porters, or by the oversnow Weasel.

Dole wrote a damning report of his own to Washington, specifying that his interest was unselfish (as indeed it was) and without interest in personalities. By dint of consultation with

scores of junior officers, medical officers, and some of the senior
officers who were exasperated with bungling, he came up with
the conclusion that bad troop morale could be blamed on bad
military management, and with another suggestion that would
give most division commanders a case of the cold grue: institut-
ing "a system for flow of ideas from enlisted personnel to NCOs
to company officers to staff." The reason, though nonmilitary,
was eminently sensible. Enlisted personnel, NCOs and most
junior officers knew more about what could and could not be
done on or off skis in the mountains than did the senior commanders.

The staff, he noted wryly, is "rank-happy, with 'rank at the top
and brains at the bottom.' " Morale, he added, was bad because
the training program was unintelligent; the "Retreat from Moscow" came about because men were neither physically nor men-
tally prepared for the conditions they encountered: "It should
have been called an exercise and not a maneuver, as no tactical
situation existed . . . and became only a test of whether men
could adjust themselves to living in the snow at a high altitude
(11,000 to 11,800 feet) under hard winter conditions. Some men
had been on skis so little that they could not handle them."

Comments from the soldiers themselves varied from tough to
thoughtful. "I love this," said one soldier, and another added,
"I'll show these guys I can take this pack if it kills me." On the
opposing side, one said, "I've marched many miles on Bataan
under equipment and the guy that designed this pack and its
contents ought to be shot. How can a man be expected to fight
when he's all in?" A final comment; "I saw boys—good, husky
boys—so exhausted and scared they deliberately stood around
and froze their feet so they could go out." Finally, Dole made
some damning comments on the folly of locating a training camp
so high that dry air and mental unpreparedness, plus the unknown factors of maneuvering in a wilderness, combined to
produce a staggering rate of pulmonary sickness and a staggering deficit in morale.

The folly of the command in forcing soldiers just arrived from
sea level to take part in strenuous exercise illustrated what was

wrong at Camp Hale. Climbers, unless they are coming back within the day, have to break themselves in at altitudes of 9,500 feet above sea level. Said Dole, restraining his temper: "The sight of normally strong men fainting during close order drill is detrimental to morale." The whole report covered eight pages, and prompt action followed.

Colonel Cochran was relieved as G–3 and made executive officer of the Mountain and Winter Warfare Board. In June, General Rolfe was relieved of his command and made Assistant Division Commander of the 71st Division. The 10th Light Division was formed from the Mountain Training Center under Brigadier General Lloyd Jones and Colonel Frank Culin, both veterans of the Aleutian war. Most important, the Army decided on another all-out effort to transfer more men into the mountain troops who would like life in the mountains.

Dole, at this time, was being driven frantic by telephone calls from irate parents, whose sons were being sent to flatland divisions instead of to Camp Hale, as the Army had promised. He decided on action. Recalling that General James A. Ulio, the Adjutant General, had a very nice Southern girl as an assistant, he asked John Morgan to take her to lunch one day. He found she relished martinis. After buying her a few cocktails to insure her cooperation, he suggested that the work for everyone would be much easier if transfers to Mountain Training Center did not have to go through her office but instead came through the Ski Patrol office. She agreed, but did not commit herself. A few days later—thanks, Dole thinks, to those martinis—the order came through transferring jurisdiction to the Patrol. He took it downstairs in the Pentagon and laid it on the desk of a friend, General Frank McCoy, who read it, and said, "I have been in the Army for forty-five years and that is the God-damnedest order I ever saw. How did you get away with that one?" Dole tactfully kept the secret until the war was over.

11

How Like a God

No ANECDOTE ABOUT THE SKI TROOPS enjoyed a broader circulation, or was more generally accepted as truth, than this one:

A soldier, marching on patrol high up on 13,500-foot Homestake Peak, picked up the voice of a pilot approaching Peterson Field, the Air Force base at Denver.

"Am at 11,000 feet," said the pilot. "Coming in for a landing. Gliding, gliding." The soldier broke in on the wavelength. "This is Private —— of the mountain troops. Am at 12,000 feet. Walking, walking."

It is a great anecdote and totally a fake. The author, Frank K. Kappler, is now an associate editor of *Life*. An editor of the post newspaper at Camp Hale at the time, he was desperately short of copy. He dreamed up the whole thing to fill space. Yet, there are thousands of former mountain troops who still recite the story as truth.

The more dedicated troopers did think of themselves as special human beings—a frustrating attitude because the post command forbade them to wear their buckled ski caps, their khaki ski pants, or any other article of military apparel that set them apart from the flatland dogfaces who jammed the streets of downtown Denver on leave. Yet, anybody with an interest in the ski troops could, at appropriate times, walk into a movie theater and see a film of the mountain men, screened at Sun Valley by Otto Lang and issued by Darryl F. Zanuck. By mid-1943, propaganda for the mountain troops was at flood tide. It was alleged to be good for morale; it was, many of the troops felt, all too good for the morale of General Rolfe. Some of his officers suspected that the publicity had turned his head as he posed, resolute on skis, the embodiment of what he thought a mountain troop general should be. In the vast confusion of Camp Hale—where orders issued by Washington yesterday were contermanded today—poor Rolfe was the butt. One night, when he stepped on the stage of the post movie theater to make a formal announcement, he was booed. Yet in the end, through one of those flukes of war, Rolfe had a hand in reducing German pressure as the 10th Mountain Division fought its way north through Italy. His division, the 79th, was part of Patton's army, advancing on the Brenner Pass from the north, and his final battle at Regensburg was against a German mountain division fighting on the Danube plains.

The superheated tone of the publicity even affected that generally conservative young man John Jay, who had become public relations officer. A November 29, 1942, release entitled "Life in the Mountain Troops" deserves repeating in part for its lush, beautiful prose:

"Camp Hale, Colorado. Ski boots crunch softly in the snow-drifts outside the barracks. It is still dark, and through the crisp night air scattered hoar frost is falling, sifting silently down on roof after roof of the Mountain Troops cantonment, high in the Rockies. From the shadow of the barracks, the trooper steps into the deserted street, pulls his bugle out from the protective warmth of his alpaca parka, and places it, still warm, to his lips. Dying echoes of the reveille notes resound among the mountain peaks overhead, then slowly fade away. Another day in the life of Uncle Sam's fighting mountaineers has begun."

That was some day, including the roster as read by Sergeant Walter Prager: Wendall Broomhall, national cross-country champion; the author, a certified ski teacher; diminutive Wendy Cram, the racer; Dyson Duncan, the Alpine climber and Peter

Gabriel, the guide; stuttering Florian Haemmerle, formerly a Sun Valley teacher; Herb Klein, former head of the Sugar Bowl ski school; Fritz Kramer and Andy Ransom, former teachers at Stowe; Torger Tokle, the jumper; Birger Torrissen, the cross-country coach; young Ralph Townsend, also a cross-country racer, and Gordon Wren, the ski jumper. Jay did manage to bring back some memories of civilian skiing—the tram station at Cannon, racing at Pico Peak, schussing the Thunderbolt on Mt. Greylock, mingled with all the classic mountain troop songs. The ending of this seven-page press release, however, put the icing on the cake as Corporal Ransom said to Lieutenant Paul Townsend: "I was just thinking, sir, we've got a combined team here that could clean up every event, if we could only enter them this year." And so the day ended for the mountain troops with the lieutenant replying grimly:

"Just wait a while, Ramson, just wait. Sure, we'll enter a team but it won't be at any Dartmouth Carnival. We've got the best team in the world right here, and the world's toughest race right ahead on our schedule . . . so keep your eyes off the scoreboard and on the ball. . . . We'll show 'em." To the accompaniment of taps and a flash of silver fire from a falling star, another day ends for the Mountain Troops.

There were moments, to be sure, but the reality of Camp Hale was rather different. Richard Rocker on May 22, 1943, wrote Dole that morale was bad in the 87th. "With certain key exceptions," he said, "every company in this regiment, in winter combat, is going to have to depend on the knowledge and experience of certain key noncoms, not on that of the officers. God help us all!" Chaplain Anders Lunde, serving with the to-be-transferred 90th Infantry Regiment, reported that the regimental cadre substantially came from Hawaii, "and they hate the place." Dole's cool reply was, "I hold little brief for the men who thought they were going to have a Sun Valley vacation and found that, after all, it was the Army." An old friend of Dole's filed an irreverent report on champion Tokle: "A washout. All he can do is yoomp. He can't ski, and he can't teach."

The help Rocker was petitioning was on the way. Some 187

men, over the spring and summer, were dispatched to Infantry Officer Candidate School at Fort Benning, Georgia, with an iron-clad promise from Dole and the War Department that they would return to the division. This led to a mathematically des-perate situation in the 86th Mountain Infantry, so largely com-posed of college men. To qualify for Officer Candidate School, an enlisted man needed a score of 110 or higher in the Army General Classification Test. When the testing of the 86th was completed, it developed that 64 percent of the men had scored 110 or higher; 13 percent had scored from 130 up, with a few of them reaching "genius" levels. In an average of 11 other divisions, only 29.6 percent of the men could have been sent to OCS. "What in hell am I going to do?" mourned Lieutenant Colonel Leo Peterson, the G–1 Personnel Officer. "I can't send 'em all." He needn't have worried. Many eminently eligible sol-diers refused to apply, for fear that, through some fluke, the Army wouldn't send them back to Camp Hale.

There were good reasons for their apprehension. The order to return newly commissioned second lieutenants to regiments in which they had served with the enlisted men was unique to the mountain troops—produced by Dole—and did not sit well at all official levels of the Army. Roger Eddy, as a committee of one, called on Dole on August 31, 1942, to report that eight new officers from the mountain troops had been ordered to Fort McClellan, Alabama. Others, despite wild screaming and frantic letters to Dole, did slip away and never came back. When the West Virginia Maneuver Area was closed on July 1, 1944, 100 of the top enlisted and commissioned rock climbing instructors were ordered to a division in the Deep South. A hasty call to Dole by Livermore led Dole to make a quick call to Washington and the Special Projects Branch, which administered the moun-tain troops. Not one of his friends was in the office. A Major Jacobs listened to him with noticeable lack of interest.

"Listen, Major," Dole finally exploded. "You don't know who I am and it doesn't make any difference to you, but I promise you this: If the orders are not straightened out sending every one of these men back to Camp Hale, I'll be in General Marshall's office within hours, and somebody's head is going to fall. And further, I am going to sit beside this phone for two hours. You've got that head start. I suggest you call me back."

"Yes, *sir!*" the major replied, and within the two-hour deadline called back to report that the orders had been changed. It was, says Dole, "the most colossal bluff I ever pulled in my life. I had as little chance of appealing to the Chief of Staff on a point such as this as I had of asking the President to intervene personally. In any case, it worked."

The enlisted man–officer situation was unique anyway. Half a dozen of the commissioned officers, including Lieutenant Paul Townsend and Lieutenant John A. McCown, son of a Philadelphia lawyer, had brothers who were enlisted men. Most of the new officers had skied before the war with at least some of the men they now commanded. There was an easy situation in the bachelor officer quarters as privates, corporals and sergeants wandered in to see lieutenant friends. Finally two orders came out limiting fraternization—not only in the BOQs but also in the service clubs, where officers were forbidden to drink 3.2 beer with their old acquaintances. At least a few of the junior officers circumvented the rule by borrowing enlisted men's caps, pulling their parkas over their faces, and sipping beer in the shadows.

The 10th Light Division (Alpine) had been activated in June 1943, with the 87th Mountain Infantry temporarily excluded because of its mission in Kiska, and with Major General Lloyd Jones as division commander. Jones, an ailing man, was hard put to weld his division together, but he did. One of the reasons was a new commander of the 87th Mountain Infantry Regiment, Colonel Paul (Pop) Goode. Goode, a hard driver and a caustic commentator, kept Dole well filled in on what was going on. Late in the winter of 1943, the division went through its D-series of prescribed maneuvers on Homestake again. Temperatures varied from 39 above to 29 below. There were frostbite cases, and some small amount of snafu, but overall the division came out with good marks from the military observers. It was a personal triumph for Goode. Corporal Wid Corn of L Company, a profane, tobacco-chewing Regular Army soldier from South

Carolina, singlehandedly captured the division headquarters. When Goode walked in to claim his laurels, to his consternation the umpires ruled that the capture was invalid. "Oh, well," he sighed. "You can't fight city hall." Later, perhaps because of his caustic tongue, he was transferred to the European theater and captured. When the war ended, out marched Goode from a Polish prisoner-of-war camp, all spit-and-polish, with a ragged but wholly disciplined band of other American officers and men behind him.

The euphoria over the D-series was not universally felt. Lieutenant Monty Atwater wrote Dole: "A lot of our best skiers, who have been in the Army long enough to know better, still haven't got it through their heads that, from a military standpoint, skis are a means of taking firepower to places you can't take it on foot. No more, no less. It's a sad commentary on two winters of work that we still can't take out a unit the size of a battalion or a regiment and move it over the snow the way it should be done." Nor was the morale improving. Corporal Ludwig (Luggi) Foeger, former head of the Yosemite ski school, stopped in to see Dole at his New York office one day, and warned:

"Don't go to Camp Hale. You'll be stoned off the company streets."

Dole did go to Hale for the D-series. One night, after these had concluded, he was cornered in a latrine by "Pop" Goode, who backed him against the wall and said, "You son of a bitch, you're the only guy in this place who can go to General Marshall and tell him what's wrong with this outfit. It's the best damned fighting crew I've ever been connected with, and you're going, and I'm going to give you the answers." These answers included a shakeup of the top command, which resulted in the retirement of General Jones from command, and the issuance of a division insignia, crossed bayonets in white on a field of blue. Dole, as a civilian, had succeeded in retiring two generals. Franklin D. Roosevelt and Harry S Truman each succeeded in retiring only one apiece.

The rumors were constant that the division would never see combat. To quash it, Dole asked for an interview with General

Marshall. He said, "Sir, why is it that this fine division has been kept in training at Hale so long?"

Marshall answered, "Dole, I have only one mountain division. If I commit it at Point X, and it turns out a month later that I need it worse at Point Y, I can't get it there. My problems of transportation are too great."

"Sir, you do believe in this type of division, don't you?" asked Dole.

Marshall summoned two aides, who carried in a relief map of Italy. He put his pencil on a point just outside Cassino and said, "If I'd had a mountain division there during the winter of 1943, when we were held up by deep snows for seventeen days, I could have knocked out the entire German communications setup in Italy. Of course, I believe in it."

The belief was not shared at Camp Hale. On June 22, 1944, the division was transferred to Camp Swift, near Austin, Texas. It was scheduled to take part in the Louisiana maneuvers in September, and the move was made early to permit acclimatization to a low altitude and hot climate. That did it. Dole was on the long distance phone day and night receiving anguished phone calls; when not on the phone he was opening special delivery letters. Division morale hit absolute bottom, and wasn't improved when—again—4,000 mules reappeared and all the new recruits had to be trained in handling them. The Louisiana maneuvers, happily for all concerned, were cancelled because the Zone of the Interior had been stripped of most units to meet the demands of the European Theater. Even in despondency, some division soldiers kept up their spirit by rappelling six stories from the tallest hotel in Austin.

Rescue, however, was on the way through a strange chain of circumstances. George Marshall had visited the European Theater in October. One of his stopping places was headquarters 2nd Division, in the Ardennes Forest. While there he met an old friend from World War I, Brigadier General George P. Hays, the division artillery commander. Hays in the first war had won a Medal of Honor for maintaining signal communications during an intense battle. Thereafter, much like Marshall, he had become an ROTC commanding officer. Hays was a percipient man. One day he advised a staff officer friend at corps headquarters that something strange was going on just across the German lines. Every night a train puffed into a station there. Try as he did with his artillery, Hays couldn't hit the station. But he suggested that heavy reinforcements must be coming in. Those reinforcements, it turned out, were for the Battle of the Bulge. Long afterward he met his friend, who said, "George, you saved my neck. I'd have been busted if you hadn't given me that information and if I hadn't passed it on."

Marshall talked briefly with Hays and, as he turned away, said to his aide, "It's a shame they can't find a better job for George Hays." In late October, Hays was ordered to report to the Pentagon—for what assignment he knew not. Flying back across the Atlantic, he stopped briefly at Iceland so his plane could refuel. While breakfasting there, he was interrupted by a tall brigadier general. "I'm Bob Duff," said the brigadier. "And you must be General Hays. I just wanted you to know you're to command the 10th Mountain Division."

Hays knew what the division was, but just knew. When he arrived at Camp Swift, even though morale was low, he felt he had lucked into something. He tightened discipline, obtained the use of a little patch saying "Mountain," which was sewed on just above the crossed-saber patch, and began intensive training. The division had never before worked as a unit. He pushed the men day and night, and finally signs of morale began to reappear. He had, incidentally, been well briefed. One morning Dole was sitting with General Clyde Hyssong in Washington. Hyssong was telling him what a tremendous man Hays was. Just then, the door opened and a lean, almost gaunt, major general walked in. Hyssong jumped up and said, "George, what the hell are you doing here?" Hays replied, "Oh, just stopping in for orders." Dole was introduced and said, "General, I'd give my eye teeth to have ten minutes alone with you." He answered, "What's the hurry. I'll give you twenty." For half an hour, as it turned out, he listened to Dole's exposition, and then went on to his new command.

On November 7, the 10th became the 10th Mountain Division, and the three regiments were given dates of readiness. All were to be overseas by January. They moved without mountain equipment. A worried senior officer, a confidant of Dole's, wrote him. Dole in turn fired off a letter to Washington. What came back was unexpected a reply from Hays. Firmly, he explained that he was now commander of the division and responsible for its welfare, "and I shall brook no interference whatsoever." Dole, who had brought about the relief of two generals, was by this letter deftly relieved of his own informal command over events affecting the 10th Mountain Division through General Marshall's office. He took the rebuff in good grace. "After all," he philosophized, "Hays is the commander. He's the one that will take them into battle, not me."

12

Even the Doughnut Girl Was a Skier

ONE RAW DAY in January 1945 a Red Cross girl named Deborah Bankart was walking along the muddy cobblestones of Pistoia, headquarters town of the U.S. IV Corps, when she saw two lieutenant colonels coming from the opposite direction. Unusual for that garrison town, they wore no divisional or corps insignia.

"Bob! Jeff!" she said. "What are you doing here?" The colonels were Robert Works and Jefferson Irvin. The last time she had seen them was at Camp Hale, when she was serving as a recruiting agent for the National Ski Patrol, traveling the country with a John Jay film about the mountain troops. Works and Irvin didn't need to explain: They had been sent overseas ahead of the 10th Mountain Division to plan for billeting and orientation of the troops. The 86th Mountain Infantry was already in bivouac at Quercianella, south of the Army's base at Leghorn. The 85th and 87th Regiments as well as division headquarters were on the high seas aboard the S.S. *West Point,* the former liner *Manhattan.* Within twenty-four hours, Debby Bankart had arranged for a transfer to the division as head Red Cross girl.

Appropriately, the top dispenser of doughnuts to the mountain troops was an expert skier. Debby had been a professional ski instructor and ski racer before the war. Once the National Ski

Patrol started out on its assignment from the War Department to recruit volunteers for the 10th, Debby traveled to nearly fifty colleges exhorting the young to join up. Her new Red Cross assignment was also consonant with the mildly incestuous nature of the division, whose inner core of privates, noncoms, lieutenants and captains constituted one mammoth ski club, where military formality was superseded by first names out of duty hours, although spit-and-polish within them. Outside this core group of perhaps 3,000 was another circle of younger skiers, fresh out of college, totaling perhaps 6,000. Added to this were some 3,000 draftees who had learned to ski but not necessarily to like it, and on the outer rim 3,000 nonskiing replacements, understandably confused by a division with as many traditions and interior allegiances as the Brigade of Guards.

The 10th at this moment, just before blooding in battle, was supremely self-confident, composed largely of men who felt themselves elite beyond any other American division. The conclusion was reasonably accurate: certainly there were infinitely more college graduates and college students, infinitely more men from moneyed families, and the only group of men in the Army who found common cause in a sport. It could even be said that the division was more elite than the Brigade of Guards, for there only the officers were, in the English sense, gentlemen, while in the 10th Mountain Division gentlemen, in the American sense, permeated every level up to the echelon of West Pointers and career officers at the top of the pyramid.

The elite of the division certainly included several dozen former Austrian nationals, almost all of them former ski teachers, who found themselves in the anomalous position of preparing for battle against former friends, relatives or ex-skiing companions in the German Army. In A Company 87th, Sergeant Friedl Pfeiffer had particular reason to reflect on the ironies of war. He had been arrested at Sun Valley on Pearl Harbor day as a "suspicious" enemy alien. Interned at the beginning in the Salt Lake City jail and then in a camp at Fort Lincoln, North Dakota, he was finally cleared. Now he was to lead a platoon, perhaps against his own compatriots from Austria.

Pfeiffer had been an international skiing champion, winner of the Arlberg-Kandahar ski races. These ranked in esteem with the Olympic Alpine skiing events and the World Ski Championships (Federation Internationale de Ski). He was a successful and popular teacher at Sun Valley, second in command of the ski school, which was under the direction of Hans Hauser, another Austrian. The Sun Valley teachers, in those days, had approximately a godlike status, and chose their wives accordingly. Pfeiffer married Hoyt Smith, daughter of a Salt Lake City bank president.

Unknown to Pfeiffer and his comrades, FBI agents had disguised themselves as skiers, going above and beyond the call of duty to J. Edgar Hoover to take lessons and to learn the rudiments of the sport. Their bag of suspects was substantial. Pfeiffer was grabbed, along with Hans Hauser and Hauser's brother, all Austrian nationals. Otto Lang, who had preceded them to this country, was clear of suspicion, as were two Swiss, Siegfried (Sigi) Engl and Fred Iselin. Just what the suspect Austrians could have done to hinder the national effort other than to boast about German might remains a mystery, but some of them did express affection for the Third Reich a little too loudly. On the day Hitler marched into Austria, according to a distinguished western skier in Sun Valley at the time, "They virtually danced in the streets, they were so deliriously happy."

Pfeiffer's period of incarceration, at least at the beginning, was considerably better than might have been expected. After all his father-in-law was a power in Salt Lake City. Iselin recalls with glee that Pfeiffer had a rug in his jail cell, and was visited daily by his wife. Things were considerably bleaker when he was transferred to the plains of North Dakota. Eventually Pfeiffer and Froehlich were cleared, became American citizens, and joined the Army. The Hausers remained in quod until the war was over.

Sergeant Herbert Schneider, of the 86th Mountain Infantry, was in a radically different position. His father, the great Hannes, was a proven anti-Nazi. Though Hannes had trained the Japanese Army during the 1930s, his talents were never used by the United States—this because his brother and assorted kinfolk were still in Austria and subject to reprisals. Now Herbert was traveling back to fight up through the Italian hills and into Austria, perhaps across the passes and over the peaks he knew as a small boy.

In another company of the 86th, Corporal Ernest Ruedinger had come back to Europe to find and eventually marry his Gerda. Though not a Jew, he had chosen to leave Austria at the time of the Anschluss. "I'll be back," he told her. "Just wait for me." Gerda was a Hollander; after Ruedinger joined the Army, she returned to The Hague and sent him her address through underground channels. Two months after the war in Europe ended, Ruedinger was given his first furlough. He hurried to Holland. He found Gerda, bloated by hunger edema, physically frail from maltreatment by the Gestapo. She had taken charge of a dress manufacturing company in The Hague, had ingratiated herself with the occupation forces, and had served as a mail drop and messenger for the underground. She finally was arrested in Brussels. "I'm so hungry," she said to the agents. "I hope you don't mind if I eat a piece of bread." She ate it, and all the written messages she was carrying. Months later, after brutal interrogation, she was released. When Ruedinger was separated from the Army in late 1945 he married Gerda, and brought her back to Stamford, Connecticut.

Not much glamour had rubbed off on Sergeant Wid Corn, one of those inarticulate southern Regular Army men transferred into the 87th at the very beginning. As the *West Point* steamed toward Naples, he was the busy master of ceremonies of a floating poker game deep in the hold. The latrine, with its slothing chemical toilets and gagging cigarette smoke, was Corn's private bailiwick. He disembarked with thousands of dollars he would never spend. Corn was killed high in the Apennines. He fitted in somewhat grudgingly with the college boys and young businessmen who fleshed out the 87th, did his duty deprecatingly, and died without mention in the newspapers. He was the typical, efficient career soldier involved in a spectacular military unit, the type of man who never gets credit for what he does.

By contrast, Private First Class Stephen Knowlton, in the 86th, had already filled books of press clippings as one of the best young American college racers. He was a freshman at the University of New Hampshire when the Army called him up, but the most skiing he was to find on the battlefront was one short, inconclusive patrol.

Sergeant James A. Goodwin, in the 85th Medics, was beautifully trained for fighting at high altitudes, a notable Alpine climber, one of the division's best climbing teachers. He never climbed a cliff in battle.

The movement of the division to Italy coincided with a long lull on the Gothic Line, the last German defense position before the rich Po Valley with its prosperous farms and heavy industry. The line stretched 120 miles across the Apennines from just north of Leghorn on the Tyrrhennian Sea to Rimini on the Adriatic. If this line collapsed, Turin, Milan, Bologna, Verona and Venice would fall to the Allies, and the Germans would be forced over the Brenner Pass into Austria. It was a stalemate by agreement. Twenty Allied divisions faced twenty-three German divisions in a sparse, barren and snowy country of jutting peaks, constricted valleys and abrupt little hills except for forty miles of Adriatic littoral. Neither side had the strength to attack. Besides, the big show was in France, where Eisenhower had taken Paris and menaced the Rhine defenses.

The war hit home to the 86th miles from the front, in the bivouac area at Quercianella. A guard deviated from the route assigned him along a railroad track, stepped on a German "S" mine, and blew himself into eternity. Other soldiers rushed to help him, detonated additional mines, and the resulting explosions killed seven men, including the regiment's Catholic chaplain, First Lieutenant Clarence J. Hagan. Five men from Headquarters Company 2nd Battalion volunteered to clear the minefields. Among them was Sergeant Crosby T. Perry-Smith. His father, Oliver, had been famous for his calm in the face of danger while making a whole series of first ascents on the rock faces of the Dolomites. Apparently young Smith inherited the same quality of nerve. He was awarded the Soldier's Cross.

The division had come to Italy almost by chance. The Department of the Army was convinced that the war would be won in France and Germany. Tenth Mountain therefore was offered first to Eisenhower. His irascible chief of staff, General Walter Bedell Smith, took one look at the table of organization and exploded: "All those mules! Hell no!" The next offer was to General Mark Clark, commanding the 15th Army Group in Italy, the American Fifth Army and the British Eighth Army. "I'll take 'em," said Clark. "I'll take any troops I can get."

Long after the war Eisenhower said to Clark, "You were lucky to have that mountain division." "Well," said Clark, "you could have had 'em if you'd wanted 'em."

The division was assigned to IV Corps, commanded by General Willis D. Crittenberger, up to then the orphan of Fifth Army. Crittenberger controlled the all-black 92nd Infantry Division, which for varying reasons had established a disastrous record in battle. He had the highly competent 442nd Infantry Regiment, composed of Japanese-Americans, the small Brazilian Expeditionary Force, three separate infantry regiments converted from antiaircraft duty, the 10th Mountain Division, the 1st Armored Division, and the 6th South African Division.

To his right lay II Corps, under Major General Geoffrey Keyes, with four divisions, and beyond that to the Adriatic the Eighth Army with another eight divisions. II Corps had battered itself bloody all late fall and into the winter along Highway 65, but it was only fifteen miles from Bologna, and the city was in plain sight. The hope of the planners was that the divisions in II Corps would make the breakthrough to the Po Plain, a fact evidenced by the decision to leave almost all bridging equipment and boats needed for a Po crossing behind that corps. It would be up to IV Corps to tie down the German divisions in the mountains. As events were to demonstrate, the aggressiveness of 10th Mountain had been underestimated.

On January 8 the 86th went into the line, into a "quiet" front. From the military base at Pistoia, where the pistol was invented, the troops could see the white gleam of real mountains. This vision so exhilarated the editors of the division newspaper, *The*

Blizzard, that they initiated a novel series of photos. Other division newspapers might print pictures of pinup girls; *The Blizzard* printed pictures of the "Pinup Mountain of the Week." One of the first was the great, gleaming mass of Mte. Cimone, cheek by jowl with the ski resort of Abetone. By January 18 the 85th Mountain Infantry was in line west of the 86th, parallel with the 92d Division, and by January 21 the 87th Mountain Infantry had begun to relieve the 86th, which went into reserve near Lucca.

In those calm days, when a battalion might be stretched across eighteen miles of front, with only an outpost now and then, the division sent out exactly three ski patrols—one on snowshoes. These were the last ski patrols of the ski troops. By mid-February the snow had thawed so much that all the fighting took place on foot. The next time the men of the division went skiing was for pleasure, and the war was over.

In the 86th, Captain David Pfaelzer, the regimental intelligence officer, decided to send out a reconnaissance patrol deep into enemy territory, covering twenty miles over peaks and through valleys, under enemy observation almost the whole way. This was a job for men who knew how to wax for crust and powder snow, how to climb on skis, and how to watch out for avalanche slopes. Pfaelzer assigned Lieutenant Donald Traynor, formerly a ski racer at Lake Placid, Sergeant Steve Knowlton, Corporal Harry Brandt, Private First Class Cragg D. Gilbert and Private First Class Harvey Slater. Through storm, inching across ledges and unstable snow slopes, the patrol made its way over the mountains at night, with a rest and tea stop for six hours at an advanced British artillery observation post. Three days had been allotted the patrol; it took just twenty-two hours, including time out for tea.

A day or two after this patrol on January 21, snowshoers were sent out to reconnoiter in the same area. Captain Bailey and two sergeants, for want of something better to do, decided to follow on skis in their tracks. As they passed a farmhouse, two Italians rushed out, screaming "Tedesco," and waving their hands. "I didn't know 'Tedesco' meant 'Germans,'" Bailey said later. "I just thought it meant, 'snowshoes.' Then the Germans let one or two rounds drop on our route and we did some real racing skiing. We skied right in the front door of one of our forward observation posts." In the 87th there was just one important ski patrol, with a few snowshoers mixed in. All those years of ski training, all those arguments about ski equipment and techniques were, in the final analysis, wasted.

What was not wasted was the "mountain sense" of the 10th Division. Men who had wintered through the cruel weather of the Colorado Rockies and had maneuvered at altitudes almost as high as the 14,870-foot summit of the Matterhorn could move with sureness in the low altitudes and generally easy slopes of the Apennines. These hills, after all, were considered merely a preliminary to the division's true role as an Alpine fighting force, rolling up the Germans back through the Dolomites to the Brenner while Patton's Seventh Army pushed southeast from the Rhine, down the Danube, and into Innsbruck from the other side of the Alps.

Josef Goebbels during the desperate days of autumn had announced that the Nazis were ready to retreat into a "mountain redoubt" of undefined size, substantially covering the Austrian Tyrol and the South Tyrol in Italy. The Allies uncritically accepted this piece of propaganda, which had no backing from the German Army. In fact, except for a few small mountain pockets in both the Austrian and Italian Tyrol, the mountain valleys were too wide to defend; the Brenner itself, so awesomely impregnable in the Allied view, was actually a wide meadow pass flanked by even broader meadows sloping up from both sides. Only Sir Harold L. G. Alexander, the Supreme Commander in Italy, expressed some skepticism.

"Suppose they do take cover in the Alps?" he said. "We'll simply surround them and starve them out." His was a minority voice. Patton, whose troops could have been used to hasten the surrender of the main German army, was secretly advised that he was to make a 90-degree turn and head for the supposed redoubt. General Mark Clark, head of the allied 15th Army Group in Italy, was directed to attack from the south. That was much to Clark's taste. He had just managed to capture Rome the day before Eisenhower's soldiers landed in Normandy, taking away all publicity from the Italian campaign. Now, instead of waiting for Eisenhower to assure the surrender of so many Germans that those in Italy would have to throw in the sponge for lack of support, his troops would be in on the publicity once again. Generals like to fight their troops, not to sit by while somebody else assures a victory. Major General Lucian K. Truscott, commanding Fifth Army, concurred with Clark on these grounds: "(1) The attack of Fifth Army, if launched in coordination with the attacks on the Eastern and Western fronts in northern Europe . . . may cause the final German collapse. (2) If we succeed in destroying the Boche here, he will be unable to withdraw to the Alps and prolong the struggle there. (3) If we sit by and wait, we allow him to continue the exploitation of northern Italy. By destroying him here, we will quickly complete the liberation of all Italy."

So the plan for the last assault was developed. While the British fought across the Adriatic plains, Fifth Army would break through the Gothic Line. This time the main push was not to be down Highway 65, where the troops of Lieutenant General Geoffrey Keyes had been battering against the defenses for so long. It was to be down Highway 64, the westernmost road to Bologna, taking the Germans by surprise. But before it could be done, a mountain had to be taken—Mt. Belvedere and its outlying peaks, which provided commanding observation for miles along Highway 64 to the north. This rolling mountain mass, where rock outcroppings jutted from the meadows, had been attacked four times and captured once before, in the fall of 1944, by the 472nd Infantry Division, but a German counterattack chased off the attackers in less than forty-eight hours.

George Hays, studying the less-than-satisfactory Italian military maps, made a discovery. Belvedere was overlooked by a steep, unnamed ridge mass to the west, almost a cliff on the American side. Unless that were taken, the Germans could deliver flank fire on Belvedere. He called in the commanding officer of the 86th, Lieutenant Colonel Clarence E. Tomlinson, and said: "Tomlinson, I want you to study that mountain face and tell me if your troops can climb it."

Tomlinson, no mountaineer, made a reconnaissance by binoculars from a neighboring hill, and reported: "It looks pretty steep, sir."

"Nonsense!" Hays snorted. "You say your men are mountain climbers. Now, let's see how good they are at climbing this mountain."

13

The Most Unlikely Way to Fight

CLARENCE E. (TOMMY) TOMLINSON was no mountaineer. He came to the 86th Mountain Infantry Regiment as commander just before its transfer to Camp Swift, and his prior service as a Regular Army officer had been in the Southwest Pacific. One of his contemporaries described him disdainfully as "a soldier of fortune," but he had a tough, swaggering attitude—and a nose both beaklike and squashed—that appealed mightily to his college boy soldiers. What they wanted was a leader; social credentials didn't matter.

Tomlinson himself found rock climbing hard going, but he knew that most of his soldiers didn't. So he sent patrols out a second time to find a route or routes up the stratified cliffs and the ice-glazed slope of the snowcapped ridge that overlooked Mt. Belvedere. This occasionally vertical but uniformly steep wall, some three miles long, was garrisoned by the 4th (Edelweiss) Mountain Battalion and the 1044th Regiment of the 232nd Infantry Division.

Not long after the patrols began their cautious reconnaissance, moving mainly at night, the hill mass achieved a name that stuck. It became known to the Americans as Riva Ridge, after a low pass that cut through its southernmost ramparts. Like so many Apennine peaks it was steep on one side only, sheared by prehistoric glaciers, thereafter eroded by wind and water. On the German side it sloped off gently, with stone farmhouses and high meadows. Military vehicles, men and mules could move almost to the summit without difficulty. To the Germans, this was easy duty in an almost impregnable position. The Americans might call the 10th a Mountain Division, but as one German mountain division officer said years later, "We didn't realize you had really big mountains in the United States, and we didn't believe your troops could climb anything quite that awkward." The descriptive term is correct. Riva Ridge is no Matterhorn or Eiger. A moderately competent climber, unencumbered by a rifle and fifty pounds of rucksack, moving by day without fear of being fired upon, could travel most of the face of Riva Ridge without the assurance of a rope. But the 86th was to move at night, in total silence, weighed down by everything from rifles to 80-mm mortars. This required the selection of routes up which soldiers could scramble, and it required careful estimating of the points where fixed rope would have to be installed to give the attackers a leg up. Patrols therefore played human fly for the first two weeks of February.

On one of the earliest of these explorations, Staff Sergeant Carl Casperson and three other infantrymen climbed a path near the extreme southern end of the face, far enough distant from the main objectives of attack so that the Germans would not be alerted. As Casperson pulled himself over the top a German sentry dog barked fiercely. The unsuspecting German on duty had his back turned when Casperson said, "Stick 'em up," and killed him. When the sound of the shots brought two more Germans from a dugout, Casperson's men got them too. The dog, incidentally, worried everyone up the chain of command to General Hays. Too many dogs could wreck the surprise of the forthcoming attack. (As Hays said, when it was all over, luck was with the 86th: "They must have sent the dogs back to Bavaria on furlough.") By mid-February, four usable routes had been scouted and green nylon rope, invisible to the German garrison above, had been nailed in place with pitons and snaplinks. These routes led up Chingio del Bure, the southernmost redoubt, up adjoining Mt. Mancinello, up Mt. Serrasiccia, the highest point, and up Mt. Cappel Buso. Lubricated by mud, broken by ledges, and in places covered with glare ice where steps had to be chopped, they were a subalpine obstacle course. After the attack, Riva Ridge was elevated by correspondents to almost Himalayan grandeur, but that was poetic license. Dyson Duncan, the transport officer of the 86th, himself a notable mountaineer, made a more accurate comment. "If you had those slopes at Mad River Glen, Vermont," he says, "they'd build a racing trail down them." Mad River's slopes are notably steep and rugged.

Cleated mountain boots and ice axes were distributed sparingly to the leaders so that the most heavily laden men could be belayed, if necessary, up treacherous spots. Most of the 800 men assigned to the attack, however, had to rely on rifle butts to belay themselves.

The original staff plan called for the holding of part of the attacking force, the 1st Battalion 86th, in reserve at the base of the cliffs. Hays vetoed this cautious proposal. "What good would that be?" he demanded. "It would take 'em three hours to get to the top, and by that time a lot of our men might be wiped out. Throw in everything you've got. Send 'em all up. Then maybe at least one column will manage to hold the top." Each infantry company therefore was reinforced to include 200 men. Chunky Captain Bill Neidner, formerly a cross-country ski racer and jumper at the University of Wisconsin, was assigned to Mancinello, and Captain Kenneth Seigman to Cappel Buso. Captain Percy Rideout, a former Dartmouth downhill racer, was supporting the attack from Chingio del Bure with Company F of the 2nd Battalion. Captain Worth McClure's Company C was assigned Mte. Serrasiccia. Elements of D Company with its heavy weapons, under Captain Erwin Nilssen, were divided among the four columns, and a detached platoon from Company A, under Second Lieutenant James W. Loose, was given the toughest assignment, the seizure of the rocky knob of Pizza del Campiano. All of these units were ordered to be in control of the entire ridge by 5:15 A.M. February 19. The schedule allowed very little leeway for German resistance, for the attack on Mt. Belvedere by the 85th and 87th Regiments was to jump off at 11:00 P.M. the night of the nineteenth.

At dusk, the huge searchlights that focused on the clouds above and bathed Riva Ridge in a dim twilight were turned off, and at 7:30 P.M., the climbers moved out. It was below freezing, and chilled sweat bathed the bodies of men cursing softly to themselves, trying to climb without having their hands stepped on by the man ahead, trying not to dislodge rocks, slipping and struggling up that endless escarpment. Sergeant Jacques Parker, a mortarman, recalls thinking he could never make it with the weight of that 80-mm mortar tube on his back. But his heavy weapons detachment hit the top and dug into snow caves in a cornice overhanging the valley without alerting a single German. With one exception, every unit either reached its objective far ahead of time or arrived unnoticed without the loss of a man. To this point, at least, it was the most successful subalpine assault on a mountain wall to take place during World War II— and the highest, 1,500 vertical feet.

By 3:00 A.M., Company A was on Mancinello. An alert German sentry gave the alarm and Company B ran into enemy mortars, machine guns and small arms at 1:12 A.M., but by 2:10 A.M. had captured Cappel Buso. Company C was on Serrasiccia by 5:08 A.M., and Company F occupied Chingio Bure at 3:55. The detached platoon was on Pizza del Campiano by 5:44 A.M., only 29 minutes after target time. The astonished Germans were able to react quickly only against young Lieutenant Loose, whose coolness prevented a disaster and caused him to be recommended for the Distinguished Service Cross. Rifle fire swept through his column of climbers before they reached the bare, rocky tip of Pizza del Campiano. The defenders rolled grenades onto them. His platoon, during thirty-six hours without food, water or communication, repelled seven counterattacks. Just before his radio conked out Loose called on the 605th Field Artillery for defensive fire.

Colonel Albert H. Jackman, commanding, asked him, "Do you realize you are asking for fire exactly on your position?"

"I do," replied Loose, "but if we don't get artillery support soon, you'll have nothing to support."

At 2:00 A.M., February 20, a torrent of shells smashed the enemy attack. Loose and his men, well dug in, were unhurt. It was 8:00 A.M. February 21 when the platoon finally drove off the counterattacking forces.

At five that evening a chunky field officer heaved himself over the top with a platoon in train. "My God!" said one soldier. "It's Hank!" Lieutenant Colonel Henry J. Hampton, who had meekly learned the arts of roped climbing from enlisted instructors at Camp Hale, had led a relief and supply column up one of the most difficult routes on the face, in record time.

That same day the 126th Mountain Engineer Battalion took only a few hours to stretch an aerial tramway up Riva Ridge, the first used in battle since the war in the Dolomites. A light cable 1,500 feet long was dragged by hand up the slopes, and a basket eight feet long, rather like the old-fashioned cashboxes in the department stores of the 1920s, was hung on. From that moment supplies went up by tramway while medical casualties, which took eight hours to carry out on litters, came down to the aid station in five minutes. The casualty rate was astoundingly low. Only one officer and six enlisted men were killed; two officers and twenty-five enlisted men were wounded.

The dead officer was bowlegged, shambling, First Lieutenant John A. McCown, son of a Philadelphia lawyer. McCown, a fine climber from prewar days, was one of the backbone men in the assault. He was carrying his father's pearl-handled officer's pistol from World War I. One of his men retrieved it; after the war, General Hays made sure it was returned to the senior McCown. Nearly one hundred Germans were captured, and the rest of the garrison retreated. The tiny number of casualties still astounds John H. Hay, then a major but now a major general. "It was a damned miracle," he muses. "A dozen men, each with a handful of rocks, could have defended those positions." Hays 3rd Battalion was in reserve, huddled in the darkness at the bottom of the ridge. Except for Company F, the 2nd Battalion, also at the base of the ridge, had no part in the battle.

One keen climber, looking forward to his first blooding, was too numbed by hepatitis to care. First Lieutenant Francis W. Sargent, later governor of Massachusetts, was evacuated to hospital before the attack began. "I was so weak I couldn't even carry my pack," he recalls. "I was beginning to wonder if I was chicken." Sargent was in hospital and out of action until nearly the end of the war.

Exuberant military commentators compared the assault on Riva to Wolfe's successful assault on Quebec, but there was a difference. The war in Canada ended when the British took Quebec. The war in Italy went on, though the capture of Riva was the beginning of the end. Nothing so dramatic had been accomplished since the fall of Rome. Of the sixteen divisions under Mark Clark's command, fifteen had been battering for months if not years against 14 depleted but still stubborn German divisions. The attack on Riva Ridge served to convince him that the mountain troopers should lead the breakthrough into the Po Valley, last reliable German source of munitions, equipment and food. Minot Dole, who had created the American mountain troops concept, was not there to see his enthusiasm vindicated. Nobody thought to invite him. He heard the news, a few days later, by way of a confidential phone call from a staff officer in Washington, and then read some censored accounts in the newspapers.

On leave to Montecatini, Lucca and Florence, an unusual number of young 10th Mountain soldiers eschewed the fleshpots to wander through the churches and galleries where frescoes and paintings brought medieval Italy to life. These were thoughtful and prudent men, no doubt a minority, who kept the division's rate of treatment at prophylactic stations notably below that of soldiers in other line units, who came bellowing out of combat and into rest areas with exactly one idea in mind. The works of art they studied in the Uffizi Gallery and Pitti Palace, the stone carving they examined on the Ponte Vecchio, all related to their battlefield in the high Apennine valleys.

For every hilltop town where carpet bombing and artillery shelling had left only gaunt tusks of stone there were dozens of little bypassed towns untouched by the curiously selective imprint of war. Gordon Dawson, adjutant general of the division, recalls such a scene: in the near distance, a church tower and a cluster of whitewashed buildings; in the foreground, peasants ignoring shelling to care for their grapes. "Wars may come and wars may go," reflected Dawson, "but the vines have to be tended." Even in February, the Apennine skies—so cold, relentless, so often pouring out drenching rain during the winter months—had an unusual tinge of warmth. But where fighting and bombing had taken place, it seemed as if Hieronymus Bosch had impatiently snatched the brush from some romantic painter to superimpose the images of death on a meltingly beautiful landscape.

This was the setting of Mt. Belvedere and its northern outpost, Mt. Della Torraccia, which lie like a stranded whale between the rolling upland valleys and the deep alluvial plain of Highway 64, curling northward along the Reno River to Bologna. Belvedere was the tallest hill mass along the line of attack, commanding observation far beyond Bologna to the gray windings of the Po. Robert Livermore, with some accuracy, compared it to low, rounded Mt. Monadnock in southern New Hampshire, the last outpost of the White Mountains above the Atlantic. Fields and wooded copses, marked by an occasional ledgy outcropping, alternated as the land sloped gently upward a thousand vertical feet to a cluster of stone houses on the summit. A narrow road pocked with German mines, with an occasional, burned-out American tank dragged off to the side, swung up, over and then down the mountain again in a semicircle.

Belvedere was festooned with minefields and heavily garrisoned. The Germans by now appreciated its importance as much as the Americans. It had been attacked three times previously and once held for three days by the 472nd U.S. Infantry Regiment. The summit had been captured in November, but the German 232d Division drove off the attackers and enlarged the defenses by bringing in elements of the Mittenwald Mountain Battalion. Colonel-General Karl von Vietinghoff, who had succeeded Kesselring in January as commander of Army Group C, the overall German command in Italy, was determined that this observation post should not fall again. General Fridolin von Senger und Etterlin, whose Fourteenth Panzer Corps had defended Cassino and now held the front east of the Reno, had earlier noted the immense significance of Belvedere. Should it fall, followed by the lower hills to the north, the Americans could move into tank country—bald, open hills—and then the way to Bologna and the Po would be open.

To George Hays, surprise was the most important element of this attack. Night patrols had scouted much of Belvedere, through a miracle passing between instead of through the minefields. Trucks and jeeps moved in along a smokescreened road from division headquarters at Vidiciatico, but the troops had to move in at night by foot along icy, muddy paths.

"There was an ungodly amount of noise," Hays recalls, "and when the attack was all over I asked one German prisoner why the defenders hadn't been alerted."

"We didn't think anything of it," the prisoner answered. "You Americans always make an awful lot of noise."

"Some of the racket came from the supporting Brazilian Expeditionary Force, which was long on esprit de corps but short on caution. Until enough frontline troops made their protests heard, the Brazilians would careen down the fog-shrouded roads at fifty miles per hour and, in bivouac, light campfires that immediately brought down heavy German barrages. In assigning the Brazilians an objective, Hays carefully gave them a minor hill mass out at the end of Belvedere and ordered them not to attack until his troops had cleared the major mass behind. This satisfied Brazilian *amour propre*, and also made sure that these somewhat excitable soldiers would not be mixed up in the main battle.

At eleven o'clock the night of February 19, while the 86th was still fighting off counterattacks on Riva Ridge, the 85th and 87th Infantry Regiments abreast crossed the line of departure and started up Belvedere. Hays, impressed by the success of the British in North Africa, had decided to emulate their technique of silent attack. Bayonets were fixed, but there were no shells in

M–1 rifle chambers, and soldiers were under orders not to fire until directed. It was a cold, clear night. A half-moon shed a pallid glow over the slopes, patched with snow, where the silhouettes of the advancing soldiers cast a gray shadow on the ground. "Scary" was the way Captain Clarence H. Swedberg of Company B described it. Yet the surprise was effective. The 3rd Battalion 85th ran into heavy fire at about 1:00 A.M., but other Germans on the ridge apparently assumed it was simply fire against a patrol. At 12:45 elements of the 87th also came under fire.

Lieutenant Colonel Donald G. Woolley, commanding the first battalion of the 85th, wryly remembers: "They told us the enemy was supposed to be short of artillery and mortar ammunition, so we shouldn't have too much trouble. What a dream, boys! Because we hadn't been able to register our artillery on enemy positions for fear of giving away the surprise, we had to go in cold. My battalion was almost blown off the mountain before we were given permission to use weapons." Woolley's battalion objective was Gorgulescu, the westernmost peak of the Belvedere massif. In the darkness soldiers blundered into minefields, and the screams of the wounded served as an obbligato to the thunder of the German guns. The Germans were desperately short of ammunition, but Belvedere was a priceless position, and they expended their shells lavishly as the two regiments moved upward. "They had everything zeroed in," says Tech Sergeant "Big Dick" Wilson of Co M, 85th. "They'd simply call in a target and down came the shells."

There were so many litter cases even the heavily wounded walked down. "Curly" Dearborn, a medic, arrived at regimental headquarters to discover that he had a charmed life. "You walked right through a minefield," they told him.

By seven in the morning and the first light of day, Belvedere and Gorgulescu were solidly in American hands but under a hail of German fire.

"That attack on Belvedere was a thousand years long," says Jefferson Willis, now a major general but then the G–3 colonel of the division. It was also strangely similar to the battle of Lookout Mountain at Chattanooga, Tennessee, during the Civil War. From daybreak on, hundreds of Italian peasants lined the hills in the valley watching the attack go on and the counterattacks come in. Gordon Dawson, observing from division headquarters, remembers it as "like a stage setting. You could see everything."

Inside the headquarters building a bloody officer staggered in to report to Colonel Paul E. Ladue, the frosty and unpopular Chief of Staff. Ladue, somewhere, had scrounged a strip of carpeting for his office, and was inordinately proud of it. "It wasn't necessary to report personally," Ladue snapped at the bleeding hero. "Besides, you're getting blood on my rug."

There were seven counterattacks on February 20 and 21, but by nightfall of the second day the Germans admitted defeat, and Belvedere was pronounced secured. Total American control of the air meant that during the daytime hours scarcely a German could move without bringing down a planeload of bombs.

Through all this fighting the Germans took only one prisoner, the only 10th Mountain officer to be captured. Morton E. Levitan, battalion surgeon of the 2nd Battalion 85th, walked right into a German detachment while looking for wounded. Introduced to a very proper German officer by his captors, he was asked: "Do you know who is really responsible for this war?"

"Who?" asked Levitan.

"The Jews," said the officer.

"But I'm Jewish," Levitan observed. "That," he remembers, "stopped the conversation for a bit."

A little later he reached in his aid kit for a cigarette and discovered he had taken his assistant's aid kit. "Damned if he didn't have it half full of condoms," Levitan said. "Imagine all the things I might be able to use and I had to find that. But it turned out later we were able to trade them to the Italians for apples to supplement what the Germans gave us to eat." Levitan had one problem. He had jotted down the numbers of the battalions and regiments and a brief outline of the battle plan, but the Germans hadn't searched him. He asked for permission to relieve himself at the edge of a stream and managed to empty both his bladder and his pockets. Passed back from command to command, he was finally freed when Eisenhower's forces relieved a prison camp in Moosburg, Germany.

One young officer wrote home from Italy expressing anxiety about the fighting qualities of the 85th Mountain Infantry. The 86th and 87th, with a hard core of skiers and mountaineers, had trained so well at Camp Hale that skiers and non-skiers were thoroughly homogenized. By contrast, the 85th had a much larger percentage of southern draftees, fed in too late to become acclimatized to mountain warfare. The officer feared that these green recruits would not only be intimidated by the rough mountain terrain but would be physically unable to keep up with the troops who knew how to move and fight in such forbidding country. It wasn't zeal that counted; it was training. In the end, the 85th proved itself, despite a slow start in battle.

Some 2,000 draftees with no mountain experience had been shoveled into the 85th at Camp Swift to bring it up to strength. George Hays and his opposite number on the German side, von Senger, agreed that mountain training made a tremendous difference in the fighting quality of the troops.

"It's a combination of level of physical fitness and a higher IQ, meaning higher morale," said Hays. "Troops not trained in the mountains have a mental block. There's a terrific advantage when you have troops who know how to handle a mountain. Particularly when you're moving at night with all the gear a soldier had to carry. That training at Camp Hale built a comradeship, a sense of reliance on one another, a feeling of cohesion that is immensely important. At Swift we had 9,000 trained men in what had been the 10th Light Division. When it became the 10th Mountain Division we took in 3,000 replacements. As a matter of fact, before the Italian campaign was over, those replacements were as aggressive as the old-timers."

Von Senger, commenting in his memoirs on the battles for Cassino—which involved far more mountain fighting than the 10th encountered in the northern Apennines—said: "For the soldier accustomed to flat country the mountains intensify all fears and demoralize him. But people living in the mountains regard them as a protection and also as a weapon . . ."

The commanding officer of the 85th, Colonel Raymond C. Barlow, was a careful, methodical officer who lacked the *elan* of Tommy Tomlinson in the 86th and the single-mindedness of Colonel David C. Fowler, commanding the 87th. His troops were slow in reaching the top of Belvedere, which infuriated Hays, but they were brave soldiers when they got there.

Worse, however, was to follow. Lieutenant Colonel John Stone, commanding the 2nd Battalion, was ordered to pass through the 1st Battalion just before 6:00 P.M. February 20 and to take Mt. Della Torraccia, the northernmost outpost of the Belvedere massif, that night. All along the ridge great chestnut trees arched overhead. German artillery fires, timed to burst in the tops of the trees, showered lethal fragments on the troops below. "Stone," said one of his officer colleagues succinctly, "ran out of steam." Sergeant Andrew Hastings, running from position to position in his platoon, was confronted by his battalion commander leaning out of a dugout and demanding that he move forward. But Stone didn't move forward himself, so his troops would not. The Germans had planted machine guns on each flank of the battalion and fired tracer bullets over the battalion positions, clearly pointing them out to the German artillery. In Company H, only one officer was not killed or wounded. The battalion was cut off from food, water and ammunition. Hays was in a fury. "The only way to get out from under artillery," he fumed, "is to keep on moving forward, and Stone won't move forward."

On the fourth day of this stalemate, with the battalion still immobilized, Brigadier General Robinson Duff, assistant division commander, relieved Colonel Stone and sent in John Hay's 3rd Battalion 86th. At 7:00 A.M. February 24 the 86th moved through the 85th. Artillery slammed in all night. Casualties were heavy.

At 1:10 the morning of the 24th, division headquarters got on the phone. "Have you anything to report? Do you need any help."

Resolute Hay replied: "Hell, no. We don't need any help here. We're doing all right."

By seven that morning the attack was over. Four German companies had attacked and reattacked the ridge. A thousand rounds of artillery had been poured in. A captive German captain was still amazed by the resistance. After the artillery barrage he had expected to walk in and take the objective without trouble. When he found the aggressive 86th still entrenched, he saw nothing else to do but surrender.

Albert Kesselring, by now back in Germany in command of Army Group South, clearly understood what the success of this mountain attack meant. The enemy, after butting at the defenses south of Bologna for so many months, had changed its line of attack from Highway 65 to Highway 64. "A remarkable division," he said of the 10th in his battle diary. Von Senger, whose corps line of defense encompassed Bologna, foresaw the result. When these Americans had moved a few miles farther north, past the road junction at the village of Tole, they would be in "tank country," where armor could move freely across the bare hills and the meadows, and the way to the Po Valley would be open.

George Hays, perhaps more than any other general in the Italian theater, had an uncanny sense of the enemy's intentions and capabilities. A gut feeling of impending victory led him to order the division into a new advance on March 3, 4, and 5. In this period the 10th swept four miles forward, moving down razorback ridges and through sunny meadows to straighten its lines in preparation for the final attack on the last defense lines before the Po Valley. It was not all that easy. Two battalions of the 85th, "back to back," as Hays put it, swept down the hilltops and took craggy Mt. Della Spe, the troops cheering as they made a bayonet attack on the final objective. Castel d'Aino, consisting of a church and a huddle of buildings, fell to the 87th. The 86th overran Mt. Terminale and, after a bitter fight, the tiny hamlet of Iola. It was in Iola that Private First Class John Parker Compton, a Le Rosey and Exeter graduate, was killed by a sniper. His grandfather, W. H. Danforth, chairman of the board of the Ralston Purina Company, printed a touching tribute to him in a message to the employees.

"John Parker Compton," he wrote, "was only a private. But a

private FIRST CLASS. With all his youth and winsomeness and courage, although he lived only twenty years, into that brief span he crowded a lot of living and made a host of friends. He filled his place with the full measure of devotion—a private—FIRST CLASS. He was proud of being just that." After the war his parents, Mr. and Mrs. Randolph P. Compton, visited Iola. Shells had shattered the church roof and left the frescoes inside open to the elements. Compton, formerly president of Kidder, Peabody & Co., the brokers, restored the roof as a memorial to their son. In this tiny settlement, far off the tourist routes in Italy, a plaque on the wall reads: "In memory of John Parker Compton. Pfc., AUS, 86th Reg., 10 Mt. Div. Killed in action at Iola 3 March 1945." Compton, like dozens of others in the division, had been offered an appointment to the Infantry Officer Candidate School at Fort Benning, Georgia. He turned it down for fear he would not be sent back to the division.

In this same advance the division's most famous soldier was killed, the only skier to be mentioned by name in dispatches from American correspondents. Sergeant Torger Tokle, the ski jumper, was serving with a platoon of Company A 86th. The platoon was pinned down by an enemy machine gun. Tokle and a bazooka gunner crawled into an exposed position to draw fire and to silence the gun. Just as they let off rifle and bazooka fire, an artillery burst in a tree overhead killed them both. Tokle accomplished his mission. The advance went on.

Midday on March 5 George Hays called Lieutenant General Lucian K. Truscott, Fifth Army commander. "We're moving now," he said. "We've got a new panzer division (the 90th Panzer Grenadiers) tangled up in front of us, but the opposition isn't bad. I'd like to keep on going." Hays' sense of the battle situation, as usual, was flawless. The 90th Panzer Grenadiers were the last reserves available to the Germans in this sector.

"Where would you go to?" asked Truscott.

"I don't know," Hays answered, "but I think we'd be able to go quite a way farther if you'd give us some aid."

In fact, even without help from Army, Hays might have broken through to the Po Plain and shortened the war by a month. The speed of his advance took Fifth Army totally by surprise, the more so because the old line divisions to the east of him, directly above Bologna, had been measuring gains in yards instead of in miles.

Impressed but unready, Truscott regretfully called back to say, "You'll have to wait, George. The rest of Fifth Army isn't ready."

When Hays was assistant commander of the 2nd Division in France, he noted that the troops had gone into the front lines in June 1944 and not one soldier fit to fight came out of combat up to the time he left in November 1944. He decided that if ever he had a division, he would give his men a chance to go back to rest areas. As soon as he had consolidated his last objectives, he sent battalions back three at a time to Montecatini, Lucca and Florence. At one point a battalion of the all-Negro 92d Division was fitted into his front line to gain experience, and he let a fourth battalion go back. An anxious call came in shortly from Lieutenant General Willis D. Crittenberger, commander of IV Corps.

"George," said his senior commander, "you've got four battalions back in rest areas. What'll you do if the Germans start a counterattack?"

"I'm all right," Hays replied blithely. "I've got that colored battalion in line and a whole battalion in reserve. If they give way I'll just run that reserve battalion over them and put the line back in place."

Such unorthodoxy made a mighty appeal to Hays' men, and so did his decision—when opportunity presented—to visit every wounded 10th Mountain soldier in the base hospitals around Florence. "When I was in World War I," he said later, "nobody ever came around to see the wounded. I decided I'd visit my soldiers so they knew I remembered them. The doctors were astounded. They said I was the first division commander ever to come see his soldiers in the hospitals. One 10th Mountain soldier in hospital told me later that, after I left, the GI in the next bed, from another division, asked him: 'Was that your general who came around to see you? Our general doesn't come around to see us.' Those visits were one of those little things that mean so

much to a line soldier. It makes him feel he isn't lost and forgotten. It's true, it takes something out of you to see those men,
so many of them maimed or crippled, but goddamnit, you're
giving something to them. And when a man's flat on his back
in a hospital, nobody will do but the Old Man."

An admiring article by George Barrett, perhaps a little too
admiring, appeared in *Yank*, the Army magazine, on March 16.
The article laid stress on the high IQ of the division and the
college association of so many of the men. There was much talk
of "an elite division" and of "bluebloods." This had unfortunate
repercussions. Tenth men on rest leave in Florence would find
themselves confronted by truculent GIs from the 34th, 85th, 88th
and 91st divisions, where the blood was less refined. "Let's see
just how blue your blood is," the non-10th men would growl,
and a fist fight would get under way. The division newspaper,
The Blizzard, printed a whole series of posed pictures of non-
blueblood 10th Mountain men registering disgust at the tone of
the article. Axis Sally, however, agreed with *Yank*. For weeks
she had been broadcasting that the 10th was composed of "sports
figures . . . sons of the wealthy." A captured document called
them "young men from wealthy or politically significant families."

The most crushing rejoinder was quoted by Major General
Robert L. Livesey, of the 88th Division. "One of our soldiers," he
wrote, "reported at length and gleefully on an incident in one of
the Army theaters. In the middle of a moving picture the show
was stopped. An announcement on the screen directed men of
the 10th Mountain Division to report to their organizations. One
of those men, while swaggering up the aisle, announced in a loud
voice, 'Guess we have to go take another hill,' and a skinny little
soldier, with the red bull patch of the 34th Division on the shoulder of his dirty combat jacket, answered for the audience, in
equally loud tones, 'Yeah, that will make two.'"

14

Over the River and into the Alps

THE FINAL BATTLES in Italy epitomized the needless gallantry of war, the compulsiveness that drives generals to commit their troops, the irresistible urge to share in a victory that could be earned more prudently by simply standing still. To everybody but Adolf Hitler and a few of his generals, it was obvious that the battle for Europe was coming to an end. Vienna had fallen to the Russians on March 8, 1945, leaving the Austrian people numbly to anticipate the end. On March 26, while the 10th Mountain and other divisions were preparing for a breakout from the Apennines into the Po Valley, General George S. Patton and his Seventh Army breached the Rhine barrier at Mannheim and, on orders from General Eisenhower, began a wild race southeast toward the Danube and the Austrian Alps. This was the beginning of the attack on the "Alpine Redoubt" that never existed save in the propaganda of Josef Goebbels. In truth the only place the Germans could make an effective stand was in the heart of the Dolomites, exactly where so many men lost their lives in so futile a fashion during World War I. No stand there ever was intended. The commanders—von Vietinghoff, Wolff, von Senger and the others controlling German forces in Italy— assumed that with maximum luck they could make a fighting re-

treat through the Brenner. Even that, as Patton wheeled southeast, was a gamble.

There were other reasons why the American and British Allied
troops in Italy could profitably have remained in their Apennine
positions. In December 1944, even before 10th Mountain arrived
in Italy, moves for a negotiated peace began. Baron von Neurath,
German consult in Lugano, on the Swiss-Italian border, had already made contact in Zurich with Gero von Schulze-Gaevernitz,
a naturalized American businessman with many relatives in Germany. Gaevernitz in turn passed the information along to Allen
Dulles of the OSS, whose headquarters were also in Zurich. The
negotiations proceeded with all the backing and filling of a
stately minuet. Kesselring was brought into the picture in January 1945. Terrified of Hitler he refused to commit himself.

Yet within weeks, as the negotiations proceeded so delicately,
Kesselring and Wolff agreed to prove their good faith by hand-
ing over two Italian underground patriots held prisoner in Italy,
and on March 8 Wolff himself slipped across the Swiss frontier
and into Zurich for further talks. On March 18 Generals Lyman
L. Lemnitzer (U.S.) and Terence Airey (British) used the same
route to confer with Wolff and von Vietinghoff in Dulles' villa.
Emboldened, Wolff moved on to Germany for a talk with Hein-
rich Himmler, by now thoroughly convinced that the Nazis were
beaten, and in early April even dared ask the Fuehrer's permission to conclude a separate peace. Hitler, dazed and exhausted,
mumbled something about getting the best terms possible but
ordered Wolff to wait before he put his signature to paper. So
the plans for breaching the German front in Italy went forward.
Originally, General Lucian Truscott, commanding Fifth Army,
had intended to make his drive straight down Highway 65 into
Bologna with the troops of II Corps, using 10th Mountain as a
IV Corps spearhead to create a diversion. He still clung to bits
of this plan by leaving the bridging equipment needed to cross
the Po behind II Corps. But the speed with which 10th Mountain had taken its high-altitude objectives convinced him that
this fresh, fast and aggressive division should lead the attack,
and he so informed General Hays.

"Who's gonna share the bullets?" asked Hays, who had merci- fully rotated his battalions and regiments so that no one unit got an overdose of bullets.

"I guess nobody," said Truscott regretfully. "You'll be getting it from both sides and in front, too."

On April 14, at 8:30 in the morning, waves of bombers from the 22nd Tactical Air Force took to the air, roaring over the 10th Mountain positions. The earth shuddered as the bombs dropped —incendiary bombs, many of them, which led Generalleutnant Gablenz of the 232nd German Infantry division to describe the scene as "Die berge in flammen" (the mountains in flames). At 9:10 the artillery opened up. It was to fire 10,000 rounds in that day and the next. At 9:40 the 85th and 87th regiments moved out, with the 86th following. Germans were rarely seen, but their handiwork was everywhere—hails of mortar shells, mines and booby traps. Hedgerows were woven with trip wires, both at foot-level and chest-high so that a soldier searching for one wire would inevitably trip the other. The division by now was being served by mule pack outfits.

"The Missouri boys loved those damned big mules," recalls David Pfaelzer, intelligence officer of the 86th, "but we figured after a while it was better to lose a mule than to lose a human life, so we'd drive them into suspected minefields. You'd see tails and legs flying all over the place."

Not all lives could be saved by mules. Sometimes human sacri- fice was required. John Magrath, from Norwalk, Connecticut, was not one of those "influential, sports types" described in German intelligence dispatches as the basic soldier who made up 10th Mountain. He was a quiet, young graduate of Norwalk High School, barely nineteen. He had skied a little on the golf courses around Norwalk and wanted to know more of the sport, which was one reason he signed up with the 10th. Magrath, a private first class, moved out with Company G 85th on April 14 up a featureless little knob titled Hill 909. His second platoon cleared the hill and took thirty prisoners. By himself, Magrath moved down the forward slope to wipe out another enemy position. Though under steady fire, he changed barrels on a German machine gun and used it to wipe out three other enemy positions. He had pushed his luck too far, however. A German shell killed him. John Magrath, whom only his platoon mates knew, received a posthumous Medal of Honor, the only one awarded the division.

That same morning in Company A 87th, Private First Class Richard D. Johnson, a skier from Winter Park, Colorado, was sent back with a message to the first sergeant. Shot in the chest, he climbed to his feet, struggled on for three hundred yards, delivered the message and fell dead at the first sergeant's feet.

Hans Aschaffenburg, a prewar immigrant from Germany, was sent out in broad daylight from Headquarters 2d Battalion 85th to map a suspected German minefield at Roffeno Mazziolo, beyond Castel d'Aino. He mapped the minefield while the Germans were digging it, called out a cheerful "Guten Morgen" to a stunned enemy, and appeared safely with his map.

By April 16 the division had broken into Tole, the last strategic road junction before the Po Valley. The attack had unhinged the connection between the 41st Mountain Corps and General von Senger's 14th Panzer Corps. The 90th and 94th Panzer Divisions had been routed. The commanding general of the 90th had fled just five minutes before the 87th entered the village. In the headquarters building a spotless German kitchen was found, potatoes all peeled, the menu for the day laid out on the table, and beside the menu a piece of bread and jam with one bite taken.

This was tank country, and fortuitously the 1st Armored Division arrived from the valley of the Reno River, blocking the roads so thoroughly, said Hays, that "you couldn't put a piece of toilet paper in between those tanks." In fact, in order to move his own infantry and artillery trucks out of the village he had to order the construction of an entirely new road. The morning of the seventeenth Hays visited Colonel Fowler. "The breakthrough has been accomplished. All regiments must keep pushing and exploit it." That same morning, with German infantry companies down from 100 men to 35 on the average, a message from Hitler arrived at von Vietinghoff's headquarters, far to the north in Bolzano, the Austrian Bozen. "The Fuehrer," said the message,

"expects the utmost steadfastness in the fulfillment of your present mission, to defend every inch of the North Italian area en-
trusted to your command." On a hill west of Tole, with the
towers of Bologna dimly visible through the haze, Colonel Tomlinson called together his company commanders and said: "Gentlemen, adjust your glasses. Below you see the city of Bologna,
the pearl of the Po Valley. When we get there we are going to
have two weeks of looting, raping and pillage. Now, let's go!"
The exhortation was scarcely needed. The whole division considered Bologna and the Po Valley a grail.

Early on April 20, the seventh day of the attack, Company A
of the 85th moved out on the valley floor and set up a road block.
By nine that night the 86th had severed Highway 9, the main
Po Valley highway from Bologna to Modena and Milan. A bottle
of whiskey, with General Truscott's thanks, went to the jeep
driver who was first out on the road. This had been by far the
most grinding phase of the campaign. More than half of the total
casualties of the division in killed and wounded were incurred in
those seven days. Bologna, however, was not to be the division's
prize. The plan of battle called for 10th Mountain to draw away
the enemy troops while neighboring II Corps came charging in.
The latter corps, however, was stuck in the last mountains, and
not until the morning of February 21 did the 34th Division enter
the city—to be greeted by a jeepload of Colonel Woolley's 85th
Regiment men who were leisurely touring the town. That same
day a briefing officer at Allied Force Headquarters, General
Alexander's command, reported: "Gentlemen, today the 1st Armored Division was thrown back 2,000 yards in the mountains
while the 10th Mountain Division is racing across the plains."

That race, the beginning of the pursuit of a fleeing, disorgan-
ized German army, was initiated midday on the twenty-first
when Hays was having a wash and a drink at his headquarters
van. "Just then," he recalls, "Truscott came bouncing in. 'What
you doing, George?' he said. 'Just relaxing,' I said. 'I haven't any
orders.' 'This is no time to relax,' Truscott said, and he bounded
off to give the 1st Armored hell for not being more aggressive.
Half an hour later Crittenberger came in. I told him what Trus-

cott had said. 'Oh, he did say that, did he?' said Crittenberger. He pulled out a small-scale map and said to me, 'Go to Bomporto and capture those bridges across the Panaro River."

Within minutes Hays had organized Task Force Duff, named for his assistant division commander, consisting of Major Hay's 2nd Battalion 86th, tank destroyers and attached units. To transport the infantry he commandeered trucks from General Ruffner's division artillery, and ordered the 85th and 87th to march cross-country toward the north on back roads, bypassing Modena and avoiding fighting wherever possible. Other generals might have been less reckless, but Hays sensed far better than other generals that the German army was a broken force. The army field manuals didn't cover a situation like this one. So Duff plunged off into the unknown, and by nightfall had taken the Bomporto bridges with only a mild fire fight or two.

What this wild chase was like was described by Robert Livermore in a letter to his wife:

"The boys have really covered themselves with everlasting glory in a bitter job, and if ever anyone won the war in Italy it was Minnie's boys. From the mountains to the plains a grinding job, from upland valley to rocky ridge routing the bastards out of their bastions and no goddamned quarter. Then I was witness to the most exhilarating experience a soldier can have, the enemy retreating in confusion. I rolled down into the plains feeling drunk with the power of the machine that rushed forward through flat, canal-crossed wheatfields, orchards and gardens— through little villages of cheering *paisans* offering eggs, *vino*, throwing flowers, cheering, 'Bravo! Viva! Libaratore! Salvi!' (saved) as they crowded around the jeep trying to touch me. Very disconcerting at 40 mph.

"Partisans were rushing around routing Fascists, firing German rifles wildly in all directions and generally confusing themselves as well as us. I will never be able to tell you the mixture of laughter, grimness, tears, scorn and joy I felt in that hectic rush, with at last the knowledge we had the enemy on the run and that we were conquerors riding through a liberated land. Then, too, I felt that these same ecstatic *paisans* would have put on, many of them, the same show for a successful German counter-attack. Yet one can't help being honored at weeping mothers holding up their children to see and wave at the *Americani* while bullets whiz about and the artillery is still crumping in the outskirts of town.

"But with 'Hail the Conquering Hero Comes' there is a horrible mixture of lilacs, roses, freshly ploughed fields and rotting carcasses. Horrid violence and gentle Spring—joy and fear—high explosives and chirping crickets are all part of it. One is keyed up beyond all thought of fear or horror or of sleep. One thinks only of the enemy, of food, and of speed against insuperable obstacles. In the morning as I back-track, an amazing sight of the stragglers of a victorious army trying to catch up with its forward elements. American troops in pairs, in groups dragging one foot after another; bearded, slovenly, with enemy pistols, with flowers in their helmets, with Italian bread bulging from their pockets, with *vino* bottles in their belts. They ride sometimes on captured Kraut trucks, in shiny black touring cars, on carts with white oxen or spirited horses, on horseback, muleback, bicycle or motorcycle, all rushing forward with tired, frozen grins on their dirty faces. Such is our enemy's rout. Such is the first tinge of victory. And ahead of it all—this great and motley column—is the advanced guard trying to keep contact with the enemy. Now I understand what it means to be the cowcatcher on the locomotive."

It wasn't all wine and roses. The division was strung out over fifty miles. Triumphal marching would alternate with short, sharp, fire fights. At Bastiglia, beyond Bomporto, Company L 87th marched into Bastiglia at 11:30 at night. Germans still walked around the town square. In the moonlight the lead scout recognized the Nazi uniform. He yelled to a group on a bridge, ordering them across the river with their hands up. Those in the square thought it a joke until one of them shouted, "Amerikaner!"

After twenty miles of continuous marching, at three in the morning, well insulated by wine and exhaustion, the men of the 3rd Battalion 87th found themselves in the middle of an unexpected battle. Tank destroyers surged back and forth through the town square. Companies K and I had joined Company L in town by this time. As the Germans fired panzerfausts the Americans retreated. The tank destroyers brought them swaying forward again, assured of American support. As these somewhat timid vehicles began to withdraw, Colonel Robert L. Works, commanding the 3rd Battalion, tore off his helmet and hurled it against one of them, and the surge forward began again. The TDs tried to hide behind the infantry, and every time a TD moved to the rear, twenty-five infantrymen piled aboard, yelling: "If you're leaving, so are we!" Officers, trying to organize exhausted men, yelled orders that nobody obeyed. A mortarman, asked why he wasn't firing his carbine, handed his mortar to the officer, saying, "Here, hold this." He fired a few wild shots and then took back his mortar. Another man, sitting on the curb and firing his rifle into the air was asked what he was doing. "Making a hell of a lot of noise, like everyone else," he answered. Captain Eddy went to sleep while receiving an order. "No wonder," he said years later, "nearly every one of us was drunk." In the gutters and against the walls were American bodies—men sleeping, not dead.

The regimental commander, Colonel Fowler, came into Bastiglia at daylight. He said to Major John McKay: "Are all these men dead?" Men lay in grotesque positions all over the square. McKay shook his head. "They look dead to me."

McKay said, "I don't think they're all dead. Most of them are absolutely exhausted."

By now Hays knew he would have to invent a new technique for moving the division forward. Even mountain-trained men could not keep up this pace. Not worrying about German counterattacks, not worrying about unprotected flanks, not concerned about what was in front of him, he ordered that his three regiments should march eight hours, ride eight hours in trucks and rest eight hours. "Artillery be damned!" he said when his artillery commander, Brigadier General David L. Ruffner, asked when he planned to be supported by shells. He did, however, carry along one battalion of self-propelled 105-mm guns. The whole division by now was strung out nearly a hundred miles from the Apennines, and in the small hours of April 23 General Duff was put out of action when a mine exploded as he was standing alongside the leading tank of his column. Ruffner took his place. Hays, riding up and down the column, found his headquarters so far back he was afraid it would be cut off. At three in the morning General Crittenberger appeared out of the murk. The division by now was just passing Carpi. The soldiers never knew it, but they were liberating the last handful of Jews in Italy's most notorious concentration camp.

"Where do I go next?" demanded Hays.

"Well," said Crittenberger, "go on to the Po."

"You've got to give me a main highway."

In two parallel columns on two parallel roads the division stormed northward into unknown country. Now and then there was a brief fire fight. Now and then, as a company halted briefly, a signorina appeared with a beckoning smile and soldiers forgot themselves for a few minutes, paying for their pleasure with wine, bread and cigarettes. To those more thoughtful it was like the advance of the victorious Goths through Italy, coming from the other direction, a nightmare compounded of shells, physical exhaustion and an overwhelming sense of triumph and excitement. What lay ahead no one knew. What lay behind didn't matter. The welcoming Italians were faceless and the war itself a blank. Suddenly, early in the morning, both columns came to a halt, but the plodding movement of Germans moving to detention camps in the rear continued.

"What you stopped for?" Hays demanded of Ruffner when he finally found him.

"There's a big river up here," said Ruffner. "It's right to our front, and I guess it must be the Po."

"It was," said Hays. "We were at a little town called San Benedetto Po. I thought to myself, 'What'll I do with these men? They're absolutely worn out with ten days of fighting and two long days of marching, and in those two days they covered about fifty miles.' So I gave orders to double-bank the vehicles along the highway, the 87th's vehicles to the left and the 85th to the right. The men were to get out and go to sleep. I woke up about 7:30 A.M. and I've never seen so many men so sound asleep in my life. I woke my chief of staff and said, 'Get those men up. I have a feeling we're going to be shelled in fifteen to twenty minutes.' The men did wake up and dig in and, sure enough, the first shell whistled down in about an hour."

The Po at this point ran gray-green with silt from the mountains. There had been an early thaw in the Alps so that the water was low. Remnants of whole German divisions had swum the 100 yards to the far shore, groping for a place to rendezvous and reorganize. The bridge at San Benedetto had been blown. Hays had no bridging equipment. It was all behind II Corps, to his right. Nobody had expected the 10th Mountain to reach the last river barrier in Italy so quickly. In fact, Hays had no order to cross.

He called in his engineer officer and said, "We want to cross as fast as possible. When will you have boats?" The engineer did some quick figuring. "We'll have boats by eleven tomorrow morning," he said.

"Well," said Hays, "have them distributed as fast as you can and we'll cross, perhaps at noon."

He was crossing into totally unfamiliar territory, with no knowledge of whether the Germans had decided to make a last stand, and with no information about the power of the German artillery across the swift green stream. No aerial photos were available, there was no air support, no preliminary artillery fire was possible, and there were no powerboats, only fifty canvas assault boats which had to be paddled against a ten-mile current. It was the wildest, most improbable river crossing ever to be made in World War II, and the 1st Battalion 87th, the original mountain troop battalion, was to lead it.

At twelve o'clock, huddling behind a dike on the riverfront, Hays turned to Colonel Robert Parker, the engineer officer, and said, "Call out to the first boats. Let's go, and we'll see what happens." Companies A and B rose calmly, boarded their boats, and began to paddle. Over their heads antiaircraft shells from a German battery concealed around a curve in the river let loose with a crack-bang sound, machine-gun bullets flecked the water, but the 87th kept moving. Lieutenant Colonel Ross Wilson, a lumberman from Kalispell, Montana, commanding the 1st Battalion, stroked his headquarters boat to the tune of an old song from Camp Hale days, "The 87th's Best by Far." Technical Sergeant George W. Hurt of A Company, one of the original glee club members at Paradise Inn on Mt. Rainier, was the first ashore. It was in every sense a tribute to the ski troopers who had served with the 87th since the earliest days at Fort Lewis, Washington.

The only German opposition came from artillery, and that soon was nullified. By midafternoon the whole 87th was across and entrenched, and the 85th was crossing. "I hadn't been back in my command post more than a minute," says Hays, "when Truscott came charging in, his boots all muddy. He'd crash-landed in a field nearby. 'What the hell are you trying to do, George?' he asked me. 'Win this war all by yourself? You know I can't support you with my other troops moving forward.'

" 'Well,' I said, 'I've got a whole regiment across there, and a second is just starting to cross. Do you want me to bring 'em back?' He said, 'No, no, don't do that. You just get a good, firm bridgehead. I'll put in some pontoon bridges.' But those bridges didn't get there for another day, and by that time we were on the way north again. Big, fat old II Corps still had that bridging equipment. They couldn't believe we'd be first across the Po."

In fact, when the 85th Division crossed a few hours later, the first soldier they saw was a startled GI from the 85th Mountain Infantry, who had survived a powerful artillery preparation for the division's crossing.

"What are you doing here?" demanded an annoyed colonel.

"Just lookin' for some aigs for breakfast tomorrow," said the GI.

It was an appropriately nonchalant comment on the ease and speed with which the 10th Division had made the crossing—the crossing of a river barrier regarded for months with apprehension by higher headquarters. In the same nonchalant mood Hays acquired himself a personal prize, a new assistant division commander of unusual ability. Colonel William O. Darby, formerly of the Rangers, had come up to see the action, having at the time no assignment. Without much optimism, Hays asked if he could have Darby in place of the wounded Duff. To his pleasure, he got him, a man who had been blooded in Algeria and had led one of the toughest of American combat units.

By this time his senior commanders had realized that Hays' unorthodox methods made sense in an unorthodox situation. Standard Army operating procedure, followed by all the other American divisions sharing in the attack and pursuit, was to delegate a specific mission to a specific regiment, leaving it up to the regimental commander to decide how the troops would be deployed.

"General Hays," said Fowler after it was all over, "didn't just fight his regiments. He fought his battalions and sometimes his companies too."

In an especially sticky situation he might call on John Hay's battalion from the 86th or Woolley's battalion from the 85th, but always when things were tense he was the man who assigned battalion objectives rather than the regimental commanders. Had his tactics been less impressive, he might have lost the moral support of these commanders, but their attitude toward him ranged from reverence to fear of his biting tongue. Thus he could move his units around like pieces on a chessboard, and whatever mission he gave them was almost always accomplished.

Task forces chosen by Hays raced out from the Po bridgehead. Woolley's battalion marched twenty-five miles during the afternoon and night to capture the big Villafranca Airfield south of Verona. Partisans reported Germans by the thousands to the right and left of the road. Flaming, abandoned vehicles lighted the night, and the dull roar of exploding ammunition dumps signaled the German abandonment of the airfield. One ME-109 pilot, however, didn't get the message. He landed in the middle of the advancing American troops, took one startled look at the color of the uniforms around him, and made his escape in a convenient ditch, leaving his plane behind as part of the spoils of war. A task force from the 86th under Colonel Darby, supported by armor, took off for Verona.

Doubts, meanwhile, assailed General Clark back at his headquarters in Florence. Verona is a walled city. Might the Germans make a stand inside the walls and force the destruction of one of the greatest collections of art treasures and medieval architecture in Italy? Finally a detachment of the 88th went in, followed by a battalion each from the 85th and 86th. The joyful mayor, half-seas over on wine, proclaimed the liberation of Verona as partisans fired off their guns and "Hail, the Conquering Hero" was repeated for the dozenth time.

Major Everett Bailey, commanding the 2nd Battalion 86th, had just settled his troops for a night's sleep when a British brigadier, complete with red hat, shook him awake and said, "Get your troops out of town. We've moved in."

"Go stuff it," replied Bailey, and went back to sleep.

Nobody in 10th Mountain had the time or energy to reflect on the state of the war north of the Brenner Pass. But on April 26, as the 10th was deciding which route to take to the Brenner, General Patton's Seventh Army took Landsberg, last city before the Austrian Alps, where a great fortress towers over the town. Patton knew perfectly well the historical significance of the Fortress of Landsberg, and paid it a hurried visit. On one cell door, in German, he read the suddenly ironic inscription on a plaque: "Here a system without honor kept Germany's greatest son a prisoner from 11 November 1923 to 20 December 1924. In this cell Adolf Hitler wrote the book of the National Socialist Revolution, MEIN KAMPF." That revolution at last was coming to an unexpected end. In two days Munich, the birthplace of National Socialism, would fall, and in nine days Innsbruck, and with it the last exit from Northern Italy to Germany.

That same day, April 26, Hays picked up his telephone for a call from General Crittenberger. "You've got to give way to the left to let the other divisions through," said Crittenberger.

"Well, where do you want me to go?" asked Hays.

"Certainly not up the Adige River," said Crittenberger. "Too many fortifications from World War I."

The Adige, splitting Verona, came pouring out of the Dolomites past Merano, Bolzano and Trento and on down in a torrent into the plains.

"Well," said Hays, consulting his maps, "do you see that large body of water on the left? I propose to go along the right side of it."

The large body of water was Lake Garda, the same canyon lake flanked by gray cliffs down which the Empress Josephine had hurried, dodging shells from the army of the Piedmont, more than a century earlier.

On the morning of April 27 the troops awoke to find themselves in the sort of country for which they had been trained, the foothills of the Alps. They were on the shores of Garda. Waiting for them were remnants of the German Army. General von Senger, ferried across the Po with his staff, had joined forces with a gaggle of troops from other divisions who had swum the Po. "At last," he noted in his diary, "we have real fortifications. They date from World War I and the Austro-Italian war." By now the 10th Mountain Division was within twenty miles of the old Austrian frontier, which crossed the head of Lake Garda at Riva.

Bardolino, where some of the best wine in Italy is made, fell without response from the Germans, but a few miles farther north, where the mountains closed in on the lake, the fighting grew tougher. This was not soldier against soldier; the Germans had lost all but their antiaircraft artillery. Of eight highway tunnels, five had been blasted. Hays, however, had prudently held on to fifty amphibious DUKWs. "Tommy," he said to Colonel Tomlinson of the 86th, "move your troops by duck and bypass those tunnels," and the 86th did. The problem was how to move the 178th Medium Battalion of Royal Artillery, giving the division close support. Lieutenant Colonel John Freeth, a ruddy-faced, mustachioed Englishman, resolved it by commandeering two big sailing schooners and transporting his artillery by water. "A full-masted ship under full sail moving toward a shore that is under hostile artillery fire is a sight not often seen in modern land warfare," noted the 10th Mountain Division artillery history.

That same day a mess sergeant, a cook, four company clerks and a first sergeant, armed only with one M-1, one pistol and four fountain pens, captured General Georg Hildebrand, commanding the Italo-German Marco Polo Division, which had disintegrated.

On April 28, the very next day, German emissaries at Allied Force Headquarters in Caserta were being harangued by Gero von Gaevernitz. "Don't you realize," he demanded, "that every sentence which we speak may cost the lives of hundreds of soldiers?" At almost the same moment officers and men of the 86th were peering out of tunnel five. At the head of the lake, at Riva on the old Austrian border, the Germans had direct observation into the tunnel. There were two loud cracks and then a shattering roar. The third round exploded in the tunnel, setting off rock fragments as deadly as shrapnel. One shell accounted for fifty wounded and five dead.

But the war was not over. Major Bailey's battalion, climbing unroped over cliffs and rocks, took Torbole from the rear. "Everybody," said Bailey later, "led a charmed life that day." All night, there was house-to-house fighting. On May 1, Colonel Darby, conferring with staff officers in the center of Torbole, was killed by an .88 shell. Sergeant Chuck Miller, a medical aid man, was watching the conference when the shell landed, blowing him through a church door.

The war, to all purposes, was now over. At Caserta on April 29 truce terms had been signed. Well before dusk on May 2 the peace was announced. Tenth Mountain soldiers took the news quietly and reflectively. Only the Partisans celebrated. One last wry touch was provided by Roger Eddy, no respecter of brass. His company was ordered by Colonel Works to take a town that lay above the head of the lake, just before the truce.

"OK, take it," said Eddy. "But don't let anybody get killed."

Works glowered, "If you had said that two weeks ago, I'd have had you court-martialed."

The next night von Senger was escorted past demolitions and down to Torbole. "How are you going to get past all those tunnels?" the German general, a former Rhodes scholar, inquired.

"Well, now, I'll show you," said Ruffner, escorting him to a DUKW, and they made an amphibious trip down the lake.

At Florence, standing stiffly at attention, von Senger surrendered the German armies in Italy. It had all happened so fast that the surrender itself was marked by one bit of confusion. After von Senger had spoken, one of Clark's aides looked at his belt and whispered to his commander, "My God, we forgot to take his sidearm!" Von Senger had been standing at attention with a loaded pistol on his belt. The pistol became a trophy of war a few seconds later.

So the war was over and 10th Mountain became an occupation force in the gray old city of Merano and all the way up the Adige to the Resia Pass. Warehouses disgorged so many bottles of champagne that the wine was free while beer cost a dime. And the 10th men, searching through storerooms, found enough skis, boots and poles to revive the sport that brought them together, high up in the Ortler range and at Madonna di Campiglio, one of the fine Dolomite centers. In mid-May their mountain war came full cycle. They were dispatched to the valley of the Isonzo near Caporetto. Where the first mountain war had ended the second mountain war added a postscript. In these crags, with their memories of the Dolomite war, the climbers and skiers moved for sport amid the tunnels and fortifications that had cost so many thousands of lives for so little purpose. Their next assignment was to have been Japan, but that war ended August 14. On October 20, under the red granite cliffs of the Colorado Front Range at Camp Carson, Colorado Springs, the division was disbanded.

In 114 days of fighting, 992 men had been killed and 4,154 wounded, the heaviest casualties of any division in Italy. It is pointless to argue whether the sacrifice was necessary. In hindsight the Allied armies in Italy might have waited for Patton, but at the time the belief in the National Redoubt was so positive that the German armies in Italy had to be destroyed. In the 10th itself there was an irresistible drive to prove the worth of mountain troops after three years and one month of frustrating train-

ing. No other division trained so long or fought so briefly. In the
end, the division never reached its ultimate objective, the Brenner Pass. Patton's troops and armor, pouring past the border
railroad station where Mussolini and Hitler established the
Rome-Berlin Axis, came ten miles downhill into Italy, met a detachment of the 88th Division, and set up a signboard that infuriated General Clark: "You are now entering the Brenner Pass.
Courtesy of Seventh Army."

What started as one man's wild dream in 1940 was still Minnie
Dole's success in 1945. His National Ski Patrol office had sent
10,634 enlisted men to Camp Hale as well as 376 officers and
graduates of Officer Candidate School. It was the only division
in any army that grew out of a sport, and the only one unified
by that sport.

15

It Was a Famous Victory

Now THE WAR WAS OVER, and Minot Dole's reward for conceiving and recruiting the mountain troops was something perilously close to financial ruin. Dole and his colleague, John E. P. Morgan, were not even dollar-a-year men. They supported themselves from their own savings or private income. The War Department supported the National Ski Patrol offices with an allocation of funds that started at $6,500 a year and eventually went up to $25,000 a year. Neither Dole nor Morgan received one penny of this. Dole did enjoy a drawing account of $7,500 per year from his insurance firm, Flynn, Harrison and Conroy, of 99 John St. Soon after the war ended he received a cool reminder that he was $10,000 overdrawn. Dole drew $5,000 from savings and borrowed another $5,000 from his bank to pay off this debt. He then set up his own insurance firm, but it was a losing proposition, and in 1948 he began to look for a steady job.

The following year Laurance S. Rockefeller hired him as chief of fund-raising for Memorial Hospital, the cancer institute. As later events demonstrated, the association was prophetic. He stuck it out for a year, and during that time raised many times his salary of $17,500. What caused him to quit was that the operating rooms were directly above the office, and he could not

stand the sounds. In the early 1950s he became an executive re-
cruiter for Ward Howell Associates, a job he enhanced through
his connection with past and present Yalies. The regard he enjoyed was demonstrated by election and reelection to the presi-
dency of the Yale Club of New York in 1958–59. During the
first of those two years half of his stomach was removed sur-
gically to eliminate a stomach ulcer that turned out to be non-
malignant. He returned, he says, to work with Howell too soon.
In 1960, after long friction with Howell, he joined Robert
Fordyce, an ex-recruiter, to establish the firm of Fordyce and
Dole. In 1964 a routine medical check revealed a rectal cancer,
just five years after he left Memorial Hospital. The wound did
not heal, and a second operation followed in 1965.

Since that time Dole has kept going stubbornly, though the
wound remains unhealed and requires surgical treatment every
two weeks. In his own words, he has been "kaput." His wife, the
former Jane Ely of a Connecticut rubber-manufacturing family,
fortunately had a little money of her own to keep the family
going.

Dole, now seventy-one, went on Social Security when he was
sixty-seven to supplement the small family income. At an age
when most men have long retired, he still hopes for a job and
a personal income of his own. The whole experience could have
been a Gothic nightmare but for the love, affection and respect
displayed so steadily by members of the 10th Mountain Division
and the National Ski Patrol. In 1963 Dole was invited to join the
10th Mountain Division Alumni Association on a visit to the
battlefields. When he said diffidently that he could not afford
the trip the Division Association put up the money for both
Doles, and did so for succeeding reunions at Vail, Colorado, and
again in Italy. On his seventy-first birthday the officers of the
Ski Patrol arranged a coast-to-coast conference call to wish their
founder well.

Now, more than twenty-five years after the war, the ski troops
when remembered at all by younger generations are remembered as part of a romantic interlude. Skiing—the operation of
ski centers and the supply of ski clothes and equipment—has be-

come a tremendous business operation. Skiing itself has prolifer-
ated as a sport. There are no accurate statistics, but possibly a
maximum million people skied before the war, many of them
only once or twice. Now there are five to six million. Where a
few thousand men climbed cliffs or glaciers before the war, probably 100,000 do so now. The climbers, more than the skiers, re-
tained their purity of vision. What Army equipment did for
them was to make climbing safer, particularly through the development of the nylon rope. What the Army could not do was
to obliterate the elements of personal skill and personal risk. But
the mass training and indoctrination brought new climbers into
the sport and prepared the way for expeditions of unequaled
daring, culminating in the first American ascent of Mt. Everest
in 1957.

The postwar growth of skiing caught even its sponsors by surprise. Friedl Pfeiffer was first to recognize the potential. Fi-
nanced by Walter P. Paepcke of the Container Corporation of
America, he built the world's longest chair lift at Aspen, thus
initiating what has become the biggest single skiing complex on
the continent.

At Vail, Peter (Pete) Seibert, ex-86th Mountain Infantry,
raised nearly ten million dollars over a period of years to develop
a mountain he used to drive past while on his way to leave in
Denver. In the East, at Sugarbush Valley, Vermont, Jack
Murphy, ex-86th, established Sugarbush Valley, which for some
years was the happy hunting ground of cafe society. Ed Link
and Roe Duke Watson, former 10th Mountain officers, created
Crystal Mountain, in the Cascade range of Washington State.
At Whiteface Mountain, Arthur G. Draper, ex-86th, took charge
of the long-delayed construction of New York State's largest ski
center. By 1970, there were more than a thousand lifts of all
types, even in such improbable places as almost-flat Michigan
and the Blue Ridge Mountains of Virginia and North Carolina.
The little Weasel was replaced by the Tucker Sno-Cat, a lumber-
ing vehicle that took Edmund Hillary to the South Pole. Now
Sno-Cats snort up and down ski trails and open slopes by the
hundred, towing rollers to beat the surface smooth. Machines

make snow when the weather fails to oblige. Skiing has moved from being a challenge to being a cinch, easy for almost anyone. John Palmer-Tompkinson, a British ski racer long ago, describes it as exactly like figure skating, only on an inclined surface.

Army records dealing with exact figures have vanished so far into storage that the Pentagon cannot provide accurate figures on how much winter and mountaineering equipment was produced. The best estimate of those formerly connected with Quartermaster production is that there may have been 100,000 pairs of skis, an equal number of ski-mountain boots, close to 150,000 pairs of mountain pants and an equal number of parkas, some of them fur-lined around the hood. Nearly all this expensive equipment became surplus after the war—pitons by the hundreds of thousands, ice axes, steel-framed rucksacks, compact little gasoline pressure stoves, nylon mountain tents—in all, more than a hundred items. They sold for scandalously low prices at Army and Navy stores. Many a 10th Mountain veteran started visibly to see girls in GI parkas and mountain pants making their turns on white GI skis.

Skiing would have grown without a mountain division, but it could not have grown as fast. The glamour of the ski troops lasted until the book took over. The Army trained a minimum 50,000 men in and out of the mountain division. Within the division at least 2,000 casual skiers became competent teachers. These men, spread around the country, served as a cadre for the civilian sport. Former troopers went into the equipment business, and moved upward with it as plastic and metal skis and safety ski bindings made the sport easier for both the experienced and the inexperienced.

Very probably there never will be another 10th Mountain Division in the United States Army. A limited number of soldiers are trained in mountain techniques at Fort Carson, Colorado, and Fort Richardson, Alaska. The concept was romantic, and fitted the times, but the times have changed. The helicopter has abolished the Army mule; the troop-carrying plane has abolished the forced marches the division made in pushing north with such speed to the Po and the Alps. It was, in its way, as romantic as the charge of the Light Brigade, though a triumph rather than a disaster. The day of the gentleman soldier in the United States Army was a brief one, never to recur. The machines have taken over. Yet in their own way "Minnie's ski troops" deserve a special act of remembrance, and this book is that act.

Acknowledgments

THE PRIME ACKNOWLEDGMENT should be made to Minot Dole, whose inexhaustible files of correspondence and documentation of the birth, growth and final dissolution of the 10th Mountain Division yielded thousands of pieces of priceless information. The Division was Minnie's creation, and it was my good fortune that he preserved a dozen filing cases crammed with documentation unavailable elsewhere.

An equally warm acknowledgment goes to literally hundreds of officers and men of the Division, who supplied diaries and provided personal anecdotes, some of which—but unfortunately not all—appear in this book. It is impossible to list all the names, but among them should be included Captain Robert L. Livermore, who kept a lucid, almost daily, account of the Division before, during and after its battles. Special thanks go to Lieutenant General George P. Hays, the Division commander, and to his three regimental commanders, Colonels David M. Fowler (87th), Clarence Tomlinson and Robert L. Cook (86th), and Raymond Barlow (85th), for the patient hours they spent in reconstructing for me the daily movements of the Division on the Italian front. Major General John Hay, at the time an 86th Battalion commander, Colonel Erik E. Wikner, an 85th Battalion commander, Captain Roger Eddy (87th), First Sergeants Walter Hard and Walter Prager (87th), and Captain David Brower (86th) are among those who supplied information of special value. I must add the names of Lieutenant General Mark W. Clark and John J. McCloy, formerly Assistant Secretary of War and Undersecretary of Defense, as well as of Robert H. Bates, H. Adams Carter and John C. Case of the American Alpine Club.

Messrs. Wilbur J. Nigh and Sherrod E. East, of the Office of Military Archives in Washington, provided a broad spectrum of military documentation. This included the diary of the 232nd German Infantry Division by Generalleutnant Gablenz; *Destruction of Army Group C,* by General Fridolin von Senger and Etterlin; the Histories of the Fifth and Seventh American Armies; and *The Battle of Bologna,* by Dietrich Beilitz (Historical Division US Army in Europe, undated); as well as the regimental and divisional war diaries of the Tenth Mountain Division.

Among especially useful source books were: *History of the 87th Mountain Infantry,* by Captain George Earle, as well as the Histories of the 86th and 85th Mountain Infantry; *19 Days from the Apennines to the Alps,* written by Sergeant Henry Moscow and published by Fifth Army; *Adventures in Skiing,* by Minot Dole (Franklin Watts: 1965); *Pieces of the Action* by Vannevar Bush (Morrow: 1970); *The Final Campaign in Northwest Italy,* published by Hq. IV Corps, U.S. Army; the Fifth Army History, Part V *Race to the Alps; Neither Fear Nor Hope,* by General von Senger (Dutton: 1964); *The Campaign in Italy,* by Generaloberst Albert von Kesselring; *The War on the Italian Front,* by Luigi Villari, M.C. (London: Conden-Sanderson, 1932); *Die Kampfe in den Felsen der Tofana,* by Dr. G. Burtscher (Verlag J. N. Teutsch, Bregenz); *Caporetto,* by Cyril Falls (Lippincott: 1968); *Invasion in the Snow: A Study of Mechanized War,* by John Langdon-Davies (Houghton, Mifflin: 1941); *The Secret Surrender,* by Allen W. Dulles (Harper & Row: 1965); and for some valuable leads on the invasion of Kiska, Samuel Eliot Morison's *Naval History of World War II* (Atlantic-Little Brown).

Though I was part of the formative agonies of the Division (I was sent to Italy in advance of Tenth Mountain and had my war on the eastern side of the Apennines with the British), I was then an enlisted man and not privy to the internal struggles that were raging. These have been set forth in lively fashion by Captain John C. Jay in the History of Mountain Training Group. He set them forth so frankly, in fact, that after Army Ground Forces had published his document, which was applauded by the Chief of Military History, it was withdrawn and rewritten to soften some of his indictments, all of which were just and accurate. Mr. Jay, since the war a producer of popular ski films, also gave valuable advice in locating photos of those earlier days.

When I was traveling over the Division's battlefront in Italy in 1965, resident Italians were helpful to me in recalling individual events, and these recollections were supplemented from the files of the Mittenwald Mountain Battalion at Mittenwald, Bavaria.

Periodicals consulted included the Division's original weekly, *The Blizzard*, edited or staffed by Sergeant Henry Moscow, Frank K. Kappler, David Judson, Merrill Pollack and Jacques Parker, among others, and *Yank* Magazine, the Army weekly.

Inevitably, where 17,000 men are involved in the confusion of war, no two see events in the same perspective. If errors have crept in, they also reflect in part the distance of us all from those stirring events, though every effort has been made to establish the actual facts. This book was written as a labor of love and in a spirit of pride for the bravery of so many of my good friends. Together they made up the best division ever to serve with the United States Army.

HAL BURTON